The Library

SCHOOL OF THEOLOGY
AT CLAREMONT

WEST FOOTHILL AT COLLEGE AVENUE
CLAREMONT, CALIFORNIA

HEAVEN AND HELL
IN COMPARATIVE RELIGION

THE MACMILLAN COMPANY
NEW YORK · BOSTON · CHICAGO · DALLAS
ATLANTA · SAN FRANCISCO

MACMILLAN & CO., Limited
LONDON · BOMBAY · CALCUTTA
MELBOURNE

THE MACMILLAN CO. OF CANADA, Ltd.
TORONTO

HEAVEN AND HELL
IN COMPARATIVE RELIGION

WITH SPECIAL REFERENCE TO
DANTE'S DIVINE COMEDY

BY

Dr. KAUFMANN KOHLER

President Emeritus, Hebrew Union College, Cincinnati

AUTHOR OF "JEWISH THEOLOGY," ETC.

New York

THE MACMILLAN COMPANY

1923

Press of
J. J. Little & Ives Company
New York, U. S. A.

TO THE

Hon. ALFRED M. COHEN

PRESIDENT OF THE BOARD OF GOVERNORS
OF THE HEBREW UNION COLLEGE

IN FRIENDSHIP
AND HIGH ESTEEM

PREFACE

Ours is an age of historical research. As the various layers of rock in the bowels of the earth have become records of geological epochs extending over untold millions of years in the history of our planet, so have the civilizations of Egypt and Babylonia, with their adjoining lands, risen out of the ruins of the past, to revolutionize the history of man, and afford us a new insight into the process of his mental and social development and growth all over the whole civilized globe. Nor can the medieval mind be viewed any longer as merely the result of the intermingling of new races and nationalities with the older ones, under the dominion of a ruling political and hierarchical power. It rather resembles a many-branched tree, whose roots and tendrils stretch out in the hidden soil into a distant spot, though, to our view, its growth appears stunted and more or less fossilized. Nor should the grandest literary product of the Middle Ages, Dante's "Divine Comedy," be judged solely from a literary point of view, as is done by most writers, particularly at present, with reference to the sexcentenary celebration of the great Italian poet, but rather as the last link in the chain of ideas and views which held sway over all the preceding ages.

In tracing its sources, we must not stop at Vergil and Homer, but take cognizance of the fact that, alongside of and behind these, there were, on the one hand, Plato, Pythagoras, and the Orphic mysteries, and on the other hand, the extensive Egyptian, Babylonian, Hindu, and Persian literature which furnished them the themes for their compositions and their concepts of cosmic life. A glance at the "Book of the Dead," that strange Egyptian Bible with its striking pictorial illustration of the hall of judgment of the dead, which dates back to the beginning of the second pre-Christian millennium, shows an affinity to Dante's "Inferno and Paradiso" which, in itself, is a subject of wonder. Neither, in fact, will the views and doctrines voiced in Dante's unique masterpiece be fully understood and appreciated, unless the reader becomes more familiarized than he, as a rule, is, with the entire apocalyptic literature of the Old and the New Testaments, from which the medieval visions of monks and priests have emanated, and which served the poet as models, if not as the source of inspiration. For, after all, Dante was not merely a poet of extraordinary versatility in all fields of knowledge of the time; he was eminently a theological writer, ranking in depth of thought with his famous teacher, Thomas Aquinas, and far eclipsing him in breadth of view and spiritual force, and it is in this aspect that he should be judged by modern writers.

These considerations have induced me to undertake this work, intended to present to a larger circle of readers and admirers of Dante an approach to the "Divine Comedy" from this novel point of view, showing, in a brief historical survey of the various lands and ages of the past, the development of the concepts of Hell and Heaven, which, together with the Christian Purgatory, form the central idea of the grand poem which has captivated the souls and elicited the admiration of the greatest minds of modern civilization.

I am well aware that many of my readers will differ with me in matters of religion when I come to give an estimate of Dante from our modern standpoint, but, nevertheless, I trust that the *nine* chapters of my book—which, by a strange coincidence, correspond with Dante's mysterious number *nine!*—will be read by them with interest, if not with profit. It is, at any rate, a contribution to the study of Comparative Religion.

Dr. K. Kohler.

New York, October 8th, 1922.

INTRODUCTION

The sexcentenary celebration of Dante's death by the entire Western world of culture has revived, as was expected, general interest everywhere in the great Italian poet, who was not merely the creator of the national literature of Italy, but who actually ushered in the modern era of literature, the epoch of the Renaissance, by using the language of his countrymen, instead of the Latin, for his titanic masterpiece. A wonderful combination of sublime poetry and profound philosophy, of theology and history, of ethics and mysticism, as this unique work represents, it has appealed, especially since the last century, to the literary men of all classes and countries as the production of one of the world's greatest geniuses, so that the Dante literature has grown to such an extent as to fill a whole library.

Yet the fact remains that it is a historical, rather than a living, interest that we take in the composer of the "Divine Comedy," because, unlike a Shakespeare, a Calderon, or a Goethe, he belongs to a world of belief and of thought we have altogether outlived. While in beauty of diction and grandeur of conception he may excel all these, ranking, indeed, with Homer, not to mention the authors of the Mahabharata, the Ramayana and the Shah Namah, we find his religious and philosophical system altogether remote from ours, however much we admire his wide grasp of history, the stern sense of justice with which he castigates vice and crime in high places and among all classes of men of his own time as well as of the past, and his glowing zeal for patriotism, for human dignity and lofty idealism, nurtured by faith. We love to quote striking lines from the "Divine Comedy," but lack the patience to read its hundred cantos. We look upon the majestic structure of this great creation of medieval poetry with the same wonder and awe that we do upon the Strassburg minster and the domes of Milan and St. Peter's of Rome, but we cannot help feeling that we are out of all sympathy with the austere medieval views championed by the poet with such earnestness and consistency, and we are lost in the labyrinth of mythological, theological, and allegorical figures presented by him. We only feel the touch of the Promethean fire which lent that unique and classical expression to the rather abstruse, scholastic system of Thomas Aquinas, in which the entire thought, belief, and hope of medieval Christendom culminated, finding it couched in the fascinating form of human striving and aspiration, and of an all-overawing, impartial divine judgment, instead of cold and repugnant dogma. Moreover, we seem to be led by the poet into a wonderland, where fact and fiction strangely intermingle, where an intense realism maps out for us every region of earth and heaven, giving us, with mathematical accuracy, the measures for the space of the world below and above, in connection with the whole known geography, and based upon the Ptolemaic system; and, at the same time, a supreme idealism allegorizes the figures of history and of religious belief, to make them types of sin or virtue, or symbols of man's fall or rise, or of abysmal wrong or heavenly perfection and love. The whole cosmos is represented as working out the divine plan of lifting humanity from the depth of moral filth and misery to the highest purity and bliss, in accordance with the decree of supreme wisdom, justice, and mercy, as conceived by the trinitarian church. Accordingly, the entire universe is mapped out in consonance with the medieval view, so as to have Earth placed in the center, with Jerusalem and Golgotha in its midst (after Ezekiel xxxviii, 12 and v, 5), and beneath it Hell, with its nine circles, the nethermost depths of which, where Satan, the fallen Lucifer, is frozen to his breast, to correspond with Golgotha. Alongside of it, Purgatory rises out of the Ocean, forming, with its nine terraces, a steep mountain, on the summit of which the *terrestrial Paradise*, the Garden of Eden, is located, on a level with Jerusalem, and above this the *heavenly Paradise,* with its nine starry circles, shines forth in radiating glory, overtopped by the Empyrean, the realm of divine light emanating from the Trinity (after Revelation xxii, 1), and having the shape of a snow-white rose, in gazing at which the beatified souls enjoy the highest bliss which divine grace and love alone impart.

Grand and majestic beyond expression as this world-aspect is, the impression of the modern reader is marred by the sad church doctrine of the eternity of Hell's tortures, which is vocalized at the very beginning in the inscription on the portal of the "Inferno" in the third

Canto: "Eternal I endure. All hope abandon, ye who enter here." The poet himself voices the "sore grief which assailed his heart" at the realization of the harsh doctrine: "No salvation outside of the church," when he learns that, however blameless and meritorious the life of the worthiest of the heathen has been, "it profits not, since baptism was not theirs." So Plato and Aristotle, and his beloved Homer are consigned to the Limbo, while it was merely Christ, through his descent into Hell, who saved the Old Testament worthies, Adam, Moses, and David, and so forth, from the same fate by carrying them with Him to the celestial paradise. Only above the vale of doom do the gladdening strains of hope resound, as the terraces of Purgatory turn the pain of punishment into pacific means of repentance, whereas triumphant joy reigns throughout the celestial spheres. At the same time, at the close of each of the three parts of the poem, the word Stelle = "Stars," is written, as if to remind us of the Latin dictum, *Per Aspera ad Astra*, "Through hardships and arduous roads up to the stars," in which the story of Hercules was summed up. The grandest figure of Greek mythology, half man and half god, Hercules had by arduous strife and struggle, by heroic combats with fierce and ferocious creatures, to make his ascent from Earth and Hades to the heights of Olympus, where he was to be ushered into the company of the gods, welcomed by Hebe with the cup of nectar which imparted to him the gift of immortality. Such is the destiny, also, of the human soul, for which the outlook should ever open to the stars above. Who knows but that some such thought was in the mind of the poet, who loved to draw his material from Greek mythology, as well as from Christian theology.

We must bear in mind that, before he conceived his glorious dream of a world beyond, Dante lived in the dreamland of romance. A troubadour of youthful ardor, he had, in impassionate sonnets, sung the praise of his adored Beatrice, whose charm and nobility of demeanor so impressed him that he applied to her the Homeric verse, "She seems to be born, not of mortal men, but of God." And when, as he writes at the close of the "Vita Nuova," "the Lord of justice called her to be glorified under the banner of that blessed Queen, the Virgin Mary, whom she held in the highest reverence," he saw her in his vision translated to the highest seat in heaven, close to the mother of the Saviour in the Empyrean. For "were not all the nine heavens at perfect unity with each other at her birth?" So was her death on the ninth day of the month in the ninetieth year of the century, as were other incidents in her brief life, proof of her mystic relation to the triad of the holy trinity—the number *nine*. "No longer would he henceforth speak of the blessed one, until the time should come when he would say of her what has not yet been spoken by any one"—such was his great resolve to prepare, by profound study, for the monumental work to be given to the world, for which the celestial Beatrice had become his sustaining comfort in sore trials, his inspiration, and his guide along the nine heavens up to the Empyrean. The strange mixture of mystic idealism and earthly reality that characterizes the "Divine Comedy" permeated, in fact, his own life, as, in his deep yearning for the supreme bliss amidst all perplexity and woe, she becomes his guiding spirit, to usher him into that superhuman state where contemplation of the divine mystery is made possible to the ecstatic soul. As reason and philosophy failed to appease his mind, troubled alike by political and personal misfortune, faith and scholastic theology seemed to offer him the ladder to the highest goal of perfection, toward which she beckoned him, who reflected for him the rays of "the Sun of divine Love, flowering forth in the Rose of divine Beauty."

The Allegorists and Mystics, whose disciple he declared himself to be, furnished him with the idea, as we shall see further on, of finding "the innermost palace of heaven inlaid with love," as the words of the "Song of Songs," iii, 10, were interpreted by the Jewish sages of old. Here we have the *leitmotif* of the "Divine Comedy," which significantly closes with the words, borrowed alike from Plato's and Aristotle's philosophy and from scholastic theology: "Love, which moves the sun in heaven and all the stars."

But, being also a classical scholar who, in common with all medieval Christendom, looked upon Vergil as the heathen sage and seer endowed with supernatural gifts, Dante chose him, the poet of the "Æneid," as model for his composition of the "Inferno and Purgatorio." In the sixth book of the "Æneid," Vergil depicted, in skillful and drastic form, the daring journey of his hero, Æneas, through the horrors of Hades, and then onward to the bright fields of Elysium, under the guidance of the Cumæn Sibyl, in search of his father

Anchises, whom he at last finds in the realms of bliss beyond the Acherusian lake, and the lugubrious river Styx, over which Charon, the boatman of the nether world, had ferried them. Here the Roman poet presents a far nobler concept of the land of shades than does Book XI of the "Odyssey," which served him as model, inasmuch as in the "Æneid" a real retribution of men's deeds in life takes place, the Cretan god-king Minos, who sits in judgment over all souls, assigning to each its destiny, according to its merit or demerit, and meting out punishments of various degrees, according to the crimes committed, whereas the blameless heroes are ushered to the isles of the blessed, there to spend a life of ease and joy. The Odyssean Hades, on the other hand, presents only the well-known three great offenders of the gods, Tityus, Tantalus, and Sisyphus, with their eternal tortures, as a warning to mortal man, and portrays Hercules as dwelling in the company of the gods, while his shade is in Hades; the rest is gloomy and, except for the figure of the seer Tiresias, primitive and uncanny. Only one feature Vergil took over from the "Odyssey," and that is the tragic fate of the unburied, who have to suffer, for a thousand years, untold woe, roaming about, unless merciful human hands on earth offer their body a resting place in the tomb with atoning funeral rites. Dante, the Christian poet, assigns a similar fate to the unbaptized, who have to suffer for no sin of their own, a view which baffles him, and which he finally accepts as faith with surrender of reason. Aside, however, from the many mythological figures of persons and monsters, rivers and localities, taken over for his "Inferno and

Purgatorio," Dante's master mind has made his poem a veritable *Sittenspiegel*, a truthful mirror of the moral conduct of men throughout history, in holding up the memorable events and personages of the various lands and ages, and particularly of his own land and time, as examples of vice and virtue, for relentless castigation or fitting approbation, like the books before the throne of God, recording, according to the Jewish view, the deeds of mortals, good or bad, as if written down by their own hands.

But what lends the "Divine Comedy" its chief value among the world's literature is the fact that it was not merely, as Carlyle said, "the voice of ten centuries," but the crowning work of millennia voicing in different languages their views of Hell and Heaven, the consummation of the efforts of the ages to espy the mysteries of the hereafter. These visions had become so popular that there was scarcely any country in Western Europe during the Middle Ages whose monasteries did not produce some saint who told, either orally or in writing, his wondrous revelations of what he beheld of the nether or the upper world in his ecstatic transports. While Ireland, England, and France especially abounded in such works, Italy, too, had its visionaries among its monks shortly before Dante's time, in Alberico, the monk of Monte Cassino; and the interest of the populace in these miraculous tales was such that we are told by the historians, Villari and Sismondi, of the fearful disaster which followed a horrible representation of Hell as shown at Florence in 1304, when, amidst the glare of flames and the shrieks of men disguised as devils, the scaffolding of the bridge on the Arno broke down, and numerous spectators were burned or drowned.

It has been said of Goethe's "Faust" that he gave to the Faust legend, which was deeply rooted in the popular mind of medieval Europe, its classic form. In a much higher degree may this be said of Dante's monumental work, the subject of which had become a matter of popular interest everywhere. For this very reason, the great Italian poet wisely chose the language of the people for his great composition, instead of Latin, the language of the Church, and he succeeded, beyond all expectation, in making it the vehicle of his high ethical and religious views. But these medieval notions can be traced to the most distant times and lands of antiquity, and it is certainly of interest, in connection with Dante's trilogy, to follow up the process of development of this large subject, through the various sources, from a wider range of view than was, for instance, undertaken by Thomas Wright in his instructive book, "St. Patrick's Purgatory," or by W. R. Alger's voluminous and critical "History of the Doctrine of a Future Life." To present, then, an extensive survey of those ideas which form the framework of Dante's immortal poem, and thereby cast some new light on its leading thought, is the object of this study.

Before doing so, it seems quite appropriate to devote a chapter to *Dante's attitude toward the Old Testament*, and occasionally cast some new light on certain less understood points. As to the New Testament, it is to a large extent based upon apocalyptic and rabbinic literature, which will be discussed in a later chapter.

CONTENTS

HEAVEN AND HELL
IN COMPARATIVE RELIGION

HEAVEN AND HELL
IN COMPARATIVE RELIGION

CHAPTER I

DANTE AND THE OLD TESTAMENT

To begin with the scriptural authority for Dante's
faith and ethics, it is noteworthy that he repeatedly
emphasizes the equality of the Old and New Testaments
as the basis. So, when he takes both to have been the
outflow of the spirit of God, and, in his creed, declares
the truth to have come to him through Moses, the
Prophets, and Psalms,[1] as well as through the Gospels
and the Apostolic writings; or when, in expounding the
so-called three theological virtues, Faith, Hope, and
Charity, before Peter, James, and John, at the heavenly
court, he first points to both Testaments in general, and
then to the Psalmist and Isaiah, as well as to God's
Revelation to Moses, before referring to the Epistle of
James, the Revelation, and the Gospel of John.[2] Again,
in the vision of the mystic chariot of the Church drawn
by Christ, the God-Man, in the shape of a Gryphon, half
eagle and half lion, twenty-four elders representing the
twenty-four books of the Old Testament march in front,
while the four Evangelists, in the shape of Ezekiel's four

---

[1] Par. xxiv, 91; 96; 133-137.
[2] Purg. xxiv, 88-95; xxvi, 38-42.

holy beasts, with six instead of four wings (after Revelation), and the other New Testament writers, follow.[3]

Familiar as he was with the fourfold methods of interpretation of the Hebrew Scriptures, even as was his master, Thomas Aquinas,[4] he was especially fond of allegorizing. Thus, right in the opening canto, the three beasts that come upon him, the lion, the wolf, and the panther, are taken from Jeremiah v, 6, and are symbols of the three destructive vices: False Pride, Avarice, and Lust; and, when he reaches Purgatory, "the realm of freedom," he hears Psalm cxiv, "When Israel came forth from Egypt," chanted by the spirits after the same allegorical method, as expressly stated by him in the "Convito."

In the midst of the circle of kings, "chief among the greatest," David is seen, "the singer of the Holy Spirits' song," and his hymns of praise and strains of supplication and repentance are echoed forth throughout the poem.[5] Most significantly is King Solomon placed among the great masters of theological lore as "the sixth light"——

> "Goodliest of all and by such love inspired
>   That all your world craves tidings of his fate.
>   Within there is the lofty light endowed
>   With wisdom so profound, if truth be truth,
>   That with a ken of such amplitude
>   No second hath arisen." [6]

[3] Purg. xxix, 79-145. Comp. Ezek. I, 4-6 and Rev. iv, 4.

[4] Purg. ii, 44, Comp. Convito Ep. x, 7. Thomas Aquinas' "Summa Theologica," on the Multiplicity of the Meanings of Scripture and the Rabbinic Fourfold Meanings called *Pa R De S*. See F. W. Farrar, "History of Interpretation," p. 95; 244 f; 269.

[5] Par. xx, 33 f.

[6] Par. x, 105. As to King Solomon's possible doom: Comp. Sanhedrin 104ᵇ, Yer. Sanh. x, 29ᵇ.

Moreover, he voices, like one of the holy angels, the deepest mystery of love's joy in Paradise.[7] The eminent place here assigned to him is mainly due to the "Song of Songs," taken by the Synagogue to be the allegorical representation of the mystic relation of God, "the King of Peace," to the Congregation of Israel, the Sulamit ("peace-lover") among the nations; and, likewise, by the Church, as expressive of the mystic union of Christ and the Church. On behalf of the Synagogue, Akiba, the great Jewish master of the Hadrianic time, said, "The whole world was scarcely worthy of the day when the 'Song of Songs' was given to Israel, which among all the holy Writings is the Holy of Holies"; [8] while Paul, in the Epistle to the Ephesians v, 32, obviously following the traditional allegorical interpretations of the Jewish masters, speaks of "the great mystery" of the union of Christ and the Church implied in the nuptial covenant. And this view has been adopted by the Fathers and Saints of the Church to that extent that there is a striking similarity found between the Midrashic commentary to the "Canticles" and the interpretation given it by Bernard of Clairvaux of the twelfth century, Dante's most adored saint.—Thus the Mosaic Law concerning the unclean beasts, Leviticus xi, 4, is used allegorically in Purgatory xvi, 103 (Compare Letter of Aristeas, 163f), and the story of Rebecca's twins (Gen. xxv, 22), in Paradiso xxxii, 60, after Paul's Epistle to the Romans ix, 10-12.

Leah and Rachel have become standing figures of

[7] Par. xiv, 34.
[8] Yadayim iii, 4.

active and contemplative life since Richard, the learned monk of St. Victor,[9] and Dante's chivalry accords to "the Hebrew dames," from Eve to Judith, the foremost place in the Empyrean.[10]   Regarding Adam's brief stay in the Garden of Eden [11] the Church Fathers share the opinion of the Rabbis that it lasted only a few hours, the day of his creation having also been that of his expulsion on account of his transgression.

Nimrod is placed among the high-towering giants, the Titans of Greek mythology who defied the rule of the Olympian god, Zeus, and were cast into Tartaros. These were identified by the Hellenistic writers, whom Josephus in his history followed, with the builders of the Tower of Babel, who provoked the wrath of God, after which ensued the confusion of their language. According to this legend, Nimrod was the leader and evil counselor. This is most drastically described in our poem, especially when some incomprehensible speech is put into his mouth, which puzzled the commentators.[12]

The most dramatic figure in the whole poem, far superior even to Milton's Satan, is Lucifer.[13]   It is derived from Isaiah xiv, 12, which according to the authorized version reads: "How art thou fallen from heaven, O Lucifer, son of the morning!"   The name,

---

[9] Purg. xxvii, 101–105.

[10] Par. xxxii, 4–15.

[11] Par. xxvi, 136–141. This strange view is based upon Psalm xlix, 24, which verse was taken to mean: "Adam's abode not in honor over night." Aboth d. R. Nathan Li; Sanh. 38ᵃ.—What Dante says in Purg. xxvi, 133–136, concerning God's Name is certainly incorrect. Dante was no Hebrew scholar, as is shown also in Par. vii, 3.

[12] Inf. xxxi, 30–74. Compare Josephus Antiqu. I, 4, 2–3 and Sibyllines I, 309–323, continued in III, 97 f. See also Geffken "Oracula Sibyllina" and the notes.

[13] Inf. xxxiv, 17–54; 81–121.

Lucifer, is taken from the Latin version, the Vulgate, which follows the Greek translation, the lxx: Phosphoros. In comparing the fall of Nebuchadnezzar with that of the morning star, the post-Exilic seer had evidently before him a Babylonian myth, telling how this most brilliant of the stars plotted, in presumptuous pride, to rise above all the stellar deities and take his seat as the highest on the Mount of Assembly of the gods in the uttermost parts of the North, but was cast down to the lowest pit of the nether world. This astral myth had its counterpart in the Greek myth of Phosphoros, the son of Eos (the Dawn), and the twofold character of the star, as day and evening star, probably gave rise to the strange myth. But the apocalyptic writers transformed the rebellious star god into a rebellious angel, and so he became either the dragon-shaped Satan or the real Seducer of Adam and Eve who is cast down from heaven. In the rabbinic "Haggada," he appears under the name of Samael, described as the foremost in rank, size, and splendor among the angels, before pride and envy caused him to plot evil against man in defiance of God, whereupon he is cast down from heaven as the archfiend. In the Gospels, Satan's lightninglike fall from heaven is spoken of as having been seen or announced by Jesus, and this story is commented on by Origen, the leading Church Father, as having been foretold by Isaiah's words concerning Lucifer. Henceforth, Lucifer has become a by-word for Satan in the Church and in popular literature. Thus Dante depicts him as "the creature eminent in beauty once," but, having been cast down into the nethermost part of the Inferno with his head downward, he offers the most hideous sight "with his three faces and six eyes looking upon the three continents of the earth, and with his bat-like wings flapping in the air to issue forth winds which cause the river Cocytus to freeze." Frozen up to his breast in ice, his colossal figure extending over the entire vertical line of the Inferno, he presents an awful picture of the demoniacal power of evil in its impotence against God.[14]

Aside, however, from all these incidental references to the Old Testament books and characters, it is its *fundamental* idea, the divine righteousness ruling all life, which permeates the "Divine Comedy." "The great, mighty, and awful God who respecteth not persons nor bribe," "the foundations of whose throne are righteousness and justice," sits in judgment over the sinners of the Inferno, to mete out their punishment in accordance with their evil doings, nor does He admit any to the realm of bliss, unless he has cleansed himself from the least impurity of action or thought by sincere repentance, while the soul ascends the steep mountain of Purgatory (after Psalm xxiv, 3 f, "Who shall ascend into the mountain of the Lord? . . . He that hath clean hands and a pure heart"), wherefore the constant repetition of the words "the eternal," "the all-searching justice, the minister of the most mighty Lord," occurs

[14] See my article "Lucifer" in the Jewish Encyclopedia; Isaiah xiv, 12-15; Revelation ix, 1, and xii, 7-10; Pirké d., R. Eliezer, Ch. xiii, xiv, and xxvii transl. by G. Friedlander, and see his instructive notes; Koran Sure vii, 11, and comp. Louis Ginsberg in the Frankel-Graetz Monatschrift, 1869, p. 150 f.; Luke xi, 8, and John xii, 31; Origen, "De Principiis" v. 5; Eusebius, "Demonstratio Evangelica" iv, 9.

throughout the poem.[15] Free from partiality and preju-
dice, the poet weighs men and nations in the scale of
unerring justice, not even sparing himself when review-
ing his life in the light of his conscience voiced by
Beatrice.[16] "The power, not ourselves, that maketh for
righteousness," as Matthew Arnold so well sums up the
Old Testament teaching, constitutes the principle of
Dante's ethics, and he, therefore, insists so positively
on man's free will, without which there can be no morality or responsibility.[17] Indeed, he is so fully imbued
with the idea of "the everlasting, living Justice" as to
be perplexed by the doctrine of predestination and the
exclusive salvation of the Christian believer, and he
only submits resignedly to it, surrendering his reason
to the dictates of his faith.[18] Of course, the Hebrew
prophets and lawgivers were concerned only with the
establishment of justice among men and nations on earth,
and they rather avoided dwelling on the state of the soul
after death, as this led the people to necromancy and
similar superstitious practices, which could only estrange
them from the true worship of God. The problem of
adjusting the relation of destiny and merit in the individual, which vexed Jeremiah, Job, and the Psalmist,[19]
remained unsolved, until the belief in the world-to-come
was brought home to the Jew through contact with new
currents of thought, such as found expression in Daniel,

[15] Inf. iii, 4; vii, 19; xi, 90; xxiv, 119; xxix, 55; Purg. xix, 115;
xi, 37: "Justice and Mercy," xix, 75: "Justice and Hope," ii, 120;
xxi, 6; xxi, 65; xxii, 4, after Matt. v, 6.
[16] Purg. xxx, 70—xxxi, 66.
[17] Purg. xviii, 49-73.
[18] Purg. xix, 27; 54-80.
[19] Jer. xii, 1; Psalm lxxiii, 3-15, and the whole of Job.

and in a late passage in Isaiah.[20]   Up to that time satisfaction was found in the simple, naïve assumption: "Behold, the righteous shall be requited in the earth, how much more the wicked and the sinner." [21]

Sheol, the Hebrew nether world, remained, accordingly, like the Greek Hades, the dreary realm of the shades, the gathering place of the departed, devoid of light and life, without any moral relation to earthly life, "the Land of Silence (Dumah)," from which there is no coming up again (= Belial), and where only "the king of terrors reigns." [22]   Only gradually the kingdom of Yahweh was extended to Sheol.[23]   It was under Persian influence that it became the realm of punishment for the soul, especially after it had been identified with Gehenna, "the valley of Hinnom," and Tofeth, the place of the Moloch fires. Also such passages as speak of "the devouring fire and the everlasting burnings" awaiting the sinners, or of "the worm which dies not, and the fire which is not quenched" [24] were then referred to after-life. Neither was the heaven, in which the stars move along the paths assigned to them, and above which God in His majesty is enthroned, surrounded by the various classes of angelic beings forming His court, viewed, in biblical time, as a realm of reward for the righteous, though Enoch and Elijah are taken up there. Nor was the Garden of Eden thought of as an abode of "delight" for the righteous after death, until apocalyptic

<hr>

[20] Dan. xii, 2-3; Isai. xxvi, 19.

[21] Prov. xi, 31.

[22] Job x, 21 f; xviii, 14; xxvi, 5; Ps. xviii, 5; cxv, 17; Isai. xxxviii, 9.

[23] Ps. cxxxix, 8, comp. Jewish Encyclopedia, art. "Belial;" Job xviii, 14.

[24] Jer. xix, 6; Isai. xxxiii, 14, lxvi, 24; see J. E. art. "Gehenna."

writers accepted the idea from Parseeism, whence the very name of Paradise emanated.

The development of these views, owing to the different historic influences, will be the subject of the following chapters.

CHAPTER II

HELL AND HEAVEN IN BABYLONIAN AND EGYPTIAN LITERATURE

A. *Babylonia*

No one can read the "Divine Comedy" but will be struck by the wonderful astronomical knowledge which enabled its author to mark the position of the various stars and constellations in the heavens above, so as to make his visionary journey up to, and along, the Purgatory terraces so real. For this, as well as for his entire view of the cosmos, he was probably, without being aware of it, indebted to ancient Babylonia, the mother-land of our civilization which gave us our science of the stars and our divisions of time and space, and also, in the main, fixed the cosmic system which held sway over the centuries down to the time of Copernicus. With so many brilliant minds of the Middle Ages, including even Melanchthon and Wallenstein, Dante shared the belief in the influence of the stars upon human life, which was likewise the heritage of Babylonia, where astrology was the twin-sister of astronomy, although the astrologers, in common with the soothsayers, are assigned by him to the torments of the Inferno.[1] Again,

------

[1] Inf. xx.

as we follow the poet in his soaring up from one celestial circle to the other, each of which he finds peopled with souls of the blessed, we see the working out of the Aristotelian lore, as adopted by all medieval thinkers, which leads us back to the seven planetary spheres of the Babylonian star worshipers, who divided the upper world into seven regions, one on top of the other, as they divided, by way of symmetry, also the nether world into seven apartments, one below the other.

But, what is of peculiar interest to us here is the remarkable fact, brought to light by the decipherment of the cuneiform tablets, that Dante and his prototypes, Vergil and Homer, had, thousands of years before, a predecessor in the composer of the grand, national epic of the hero Gilgames, the king and builder of the ancient city of Erech, who, after his many bold deeds, ventured out on a daring voyage across the Arabian desert, the wide Western ocean, and finally, across the dark "waters of death" in search of Parnapishtim, the very wise (Chasisadra = Xisuthros), the Babylonian Noah, enjoying a beatified life on a paradiselike island at the confluence of the rivers Euphrates and Tigris on the shore of the Persian gulf. In twelve chapters, corresponding to the twelve months of the year, his heroic deeds, partly resembling those of Hercules, are told. We need not dwell on the half historical, half mythological tales presented in the former fragmentary part of the epic. Our interest lies in the latter half, describing his march along "the difficult road never trod by mortal man before," first through a wilderness beset by lions, then through the mountains of Mashu, "whose summit touches the dome of heaven, and whose breast reaches down to Aralu (Hades), the entrance to which is guarded by scorpionlike monsters. Dense darkness envelops the wanderer, until he comes to a wondrous park of the gods, where, as in Ezekiel's Eden (xxviii, 13), precious stones hang down from the trees like clusters of grapes. On reaching "the sea which encircles the earth," he encounters the goddess Siduri of Sabu (= Sheba), enthroned in her palace on the shore. She directs him to find the boatman of Parnapishtim and to be ferried by him over the dangerous sea and the waters of death, where the Babylonian Charon acts as boatman. At last he comes within sight of his ancestor, the hero of the flood, whose tale is given in almost the same language as the biblical account. But he fails to attain the real object of his great venture, for he learns that the coveted boon of immortality is denied to man. Neither gods nor men can help him to escape the inexorable law of mortality. He is cured of the dreadful disease inflicted on him by the angry goddess, Ishtar, as he bathes in the miraculous "fountain of purification" at the advice of Parnapishtim. Moreover, owing to the help of the latter's wife, he becomes possessor of the magic plant of life's rejuvenation that grows near by, but fate decrees that a demon, in the shape of a serpent, snatches it away, and he has to return home sorely disappointed. Still he craves to know what the lot of the dead is, and with the help of Nergal,[2] the god of the dead, he conjures up the spirit of his departed friend, Eabani. From him he learns

[2] II Kings xxiii.

that "heroes slain in battle find rest on their couches below, when provided with water and food, after having been honored by proper funeral rites, whereas he whose body lies forsaken in the field, and whose ghost has none to care for him, is doomed to restlessness and consumed by ever-gnawing hunger." We thus meet here with the same view concerning the misery of the unburied as is experienced by the unfortunate in Hades, according to the "Odyssey" and the "Æneid."

The dreary character of the nether world and the cheerless outlook upon the hereafter, reflected also in the ancient Hebrew literature, as we have seen above, find expression, especially, in the descent of Ishtar into Hades, made familiar to the laic world of to-day by the work of the French composer, Vincent d'Indy, and others. Obviously, an original nature myth, like that of Demeter and Persephone, if not also of Orpheus and Eurydice, depicting the vanishing of fertility on earth at the turn of the summer season, the poem describes Ishtar's going down to the nether world, "the land whence there is no return." At each of the seven gates she is, at the command of the fierce goddess residing in the interior, stripped of a part of her ornaments and clothing, until she appears naked before the relentless queen of Hades, to be imprisoned there; whereupon all productivity among beasts and men ceases, and the gods above lament her disappearance. Only at the interference of the powerful god, Ea, is she released; and after she has been sprinkled with the "water of life," she is led out again through the seven gates, at each of which the one or the other part of her garments is restored, as she goes up. In another myth the number of gates is twice the number seven, and as many messengers of death are at the disposal of the ruler of Hades, while a guardian announces all newcomers to her, allowing none to pass beyond the bars and bolts of the "house of darkness." There they find: "Dust is their nourishment, their food, clay; they are clothed, like birds, in a garment of feathers, forever deprived of light."

Still gloomier is the aspect of the Babylonian Hades, as we glance at its pictorial representation, presenting the terrific dog-shaped monster, the original Cerberus, surveying Hades, and the fierce lion-headed goddess, Allatu, holding serpents in her hands, and terrific monsters upon her breast, while she kneels on a horse in a boat floating along the "river of death."

Nor is reference made anywhere to a paradisiacal abode of bliss for the privileged souls of the good. The thought of retribution, or of a judgment in the hereafter, as far as we can see, did not occur to the Babylonian or ancient Semitic mind. The fate of all those in Hades or Aralu (compare Ezek. xxxii, 18-32) is the same. Looking up to the stars as life's rulers, the Babylonians beheld, in their sun god, the judge and lawgiver of mankind, from whom the king, Hammurabi, in Abraham's time, received the laws he had codified, as did Moses from the God, Yahweh. To the nether world the sun god's dominion did not extend. Neither did Yahweh originally reign over Sheol. Only at a very late period was His omnipresence proclaimed by the Psalmist:

"If I mount to heaven, Thou art there;
If I make Sheol my couch, Thou art there." [3]

Especially was the hopelessness of man's yearning and striving for a life of the gods brought out in two characteristic legends. The one tells of Etana (possibly identical with the biblical Ethan, one of the wise men of the East in I Kings v, 11, as suggested by Jastrow), who attempted to fly to the heavenly abodes at the instigation of an eagle, his friend, on whose breast he was lying. On rising higher and higher, he beheld the earth beneath as if it were a mountain, and the sea as if it were a mere gardener's ditch (compare a similar Alexander legend in the Talmud Yer. Ab. Zara iii, 42c)—but when he came as far as the dwelling of Anu, the god of heaven, he, together with the eagle, was hurled down to become a dweller of Hades. [4] The other legend relates the story of Adapa, the favorite son of the god, Ea, the father of mankind, who was endowed with the wisdom and knowledge of the gods. But as he had entered the interior of heaven and was about to partake of the food of the gods, he was prevented by some deceptive trick of the jealous god, Ea, from so doing, and he had to forego the boon of immortality. [5] Here we have the parallel to the Hebrew legend of Adam, who, after he had eaten of the tree of knowledge, was expelled from the Garden of Eden, lest he eat also of the tree of life, and be like the deathless gods. Man's

[3] Ps. cxxxix, 8.
[4] Jastrow, "Religion of Assyria and Babylonia," p. 519; Sayce, "The Religion of the Ancient Egypt and Babylonia," p. 425 f.
[5] Jastrow *l. c.,* 544 f; Sayce *l. c.,* 383 f.

destiny is to live on earth; beyond this—such was the ancient Semitic view—the shadowy existence of the ghosts—Rephaim—awaits him in the infernal regions, to which only necromancy—the survival of primitive animism—gave the semblance of life, to satisfy the curiosity of the blind masses. The higher spiritual view, which beholds man as a personality made in the image of God, who with mind and soul craves to partake in His divine nature, was, of course, beyond the reach of those remote ages.

B. *Egypt*

Of greater importance than the discoveries made by modern research in the Euphrates valley are, for our subject, the revelations that have come to us from the land of the Nile. The mystery which formerly surrounded this ancient center of civilization, with its colossal pyramids and sphinxes and its strange hieroglyphics, is no longer hidden from us. Modern scholars have lifted the veil from a past dating back to six or seven thousand years ago, and we now see, in the dim twilight of history, the process of development of a people composed of Asiatic and African races, of fetish and animal worshipers, and of worshipers of solar deities in the shape and of the character of human beings. Different from the Babylonian Semites who, when invading the land of Shinar (= Sumer?), found a non-Semitic population already in possession of culture, such as is indicated by the invention of the cuneiform picture writing, the aborigines of Egypt belonged to the primitive African race who beheld in beast, bird, or plant, according to their useful or fearful character, divine or demoniacal beings. In merging with them, the Asiatic invaders learned to worship these also, and gradually, by way of symbolism, combined the animal with the human shape of their deities, reserving the pure human form for the solar gods. Thus the prehistoric views and practices were tenaciously adhered to by the people, while the kings, the deified Pharaohs, fostered more and more the priestly cult of the solar man-god, in whose honor they erected the obelisks, pointing like fingers to the heaven above. For the preservation of their bodies they built the pyramidal sepulchers and had them guarded by majestic sphinxes, counterparts of the cherubs that guarded the temples and palaces of the Babylonian kings. It was the soul, the "double," which was to outlast life that became the chief object of their solicitude.[6] Henceforth, the daily setting of the sun god, Ra, beneath the Western horizon, and his rising anew in the East on the following morning, became, to king and people, the dramatic picture of human life. As they beheld him sailing along the heaven in his bark, until, on reaching the Western end, he would sink into the *Amenti*, the realm of the dead beneath, to rise again on the other end as a new god— Tum or Horus, so man journeys along on earth, until he goes down to the dark world below, a prey to the hostile powers of the deep. Should he not, then, like-

[6] See for all the following: Sayce *l. c.*, p. 153-251; Tiele, "Egyptian Religion" and art., "Egypt" by Flinders Petrie, in Encyclopedia of Religion and Ethics; Wiedeman, "Religion der Aegypter"; Maspero, "Dawn of Civilization," p. 190 f.

wise undergo a renewal, so that the nether world becomes to him "the house of life?" In this hope the Egyptians buried their dead in the Western part of their cities, and, believing in the continuance of the soul, or "double," for the protection of which they resorted to all sorts of magical practices, they were the first to develop the doctrine of the immortality of the soul. But it was chiefly on the ancient god, Osiris, of Asiatic origin, who, owing to his appealing human qualities, became the most popular deity of the land, that the idea of immortality was from the earliest time centered. Son of the most ancient gods in the Egyptian pantheon, the god of the earth and the queen of the ocean, Osiris, with the surname, "the beneficent being," was looked upon as the first king and benefactor of men, the first to be mummified, and the first to rise from the dead, a pattern to mortal man to strive for goodness and beneficence like him and become Osiris himself. Upon attaining this goal in afterlife, and escaping thereby all the horrors and hostile attacks of the fiends and monsters of the world beneath, the thought and lifelong toil of the Egyptian were bent; yet, at the same time, innumerable magic formulas and amulets were resorted to, to ward off the threatening powers. To this end, the coffins and pyramidal sepulchers were made the depositaries of endless prayers and incantations and similar writings, and to this practice we owe the preservation of the entire sacred literature of Egypt, foremost among which is the famous "Book of the Dead," with its one hundred and sixty-five chapters, collected in different order and versions in the course of centuries, and supposed to have been recited, or used, as the means of protection or salvation of the soul of the dead. Under the mystic title, "The Going Forth by Day," the various chapters describe the conflict waged by either Ra or Osiris with the infernal foes, until the final triumph was attained, and by emulating the god, the soul merged into Osiris was to obtain salvation and be admitted into the *fields of Alu* (= *the "Elysian Fields"*), where a life without pain or death, an abundant harvest, with six-ells-high stalks of corn under an eternal sunshine and mild zephyr winds, await the blessed toiler. In the older chapters of the book the mythical and magic elements conditioning the triumph of the god and the rescue of the soul prevail, but later on, the ethical view of life is more and more accentuated, until the climax is reached in the one hundred and twenty-fifth chapter, which forms the high mark of the whole literature, and which, considering the time and environment, shows a surprisingly high standard of ethics. It portrays in impressive words and in a magnificent illustration in colors the ushering in of the dead—that his, his "double"—by Maat, the goddess of truth and justice, into the Hall of Judgment, presided over by Osiris, the judge of the nether world. He is surrounded by forty-two assessors—corresponding to the forty-two districts of the land—who are seated on the canopy above the throne, each having an ostrich feather, symbol of the twofold truth, on his head. Before Osiris' throne, the four genii of the dead are seen emerging, amidst lotus flowers, from "the waters of life." Near by, Anubis, the conductor and guardian of the dead, and

Horus, the younger sun god, both sons of Osiris, are seen weighing the heart of the dead in the scales against an ostrich feather, while a dog-headed figure, representing correct measurement, lies on top of the scales watching. The ibis-headed god, Thoth, the heavenly recorder, writes down the result on his papyrus. But, first of all, the dead person, with one hand lifted up to heaven and the other held against the seat of his heart, makes his confession, kneeling before the forty-two assistant judges, declaring that he did not commit any of the forty-two sins over which each of these judges holds specific and relentless jurisdiction. He then addresses them saying:

"Homage to you, masters of truth. Homage to thee, great god, the master of truth! I have come before thee. I know thy name and the names of the forty-two gods who are with thee in the Hall of the Two Truths (truth and justice), who live on taking hold of sinners, and feed upon their blood on the day of reckoning before the beneficent being (= Osiris).

> "Now, double soul, mistress of truth, I bring you truth, and I keep from you the wrong (= falsehood):
> I have not done any harm or malice to any man.
> I have not oppressed kinsmen (the poor, or the widow).
> I have not lied at court.
> I have not robbed men.
> I have not been a slayer of men.
> I have not stinted the quantity of corn.
> I have not seized the property of the gods.

I have not monopolized food.
I have not been an extortioner.
I have not been unchaste with women or with men.
I have not exacted more work from the laborer than was just.
I have not caused the slave to be illtreated by his master.
I have not made any one to hunger.
I have made none to weep.
I have not been a teller of lies.
I have not caused any man to be treacherously murdered.
'I have not been a doer of violence.
'I have not pillaged cultivated lands.
'I have not been a slanderer.
I have not been quarrelsome.
'I have not been a revoker of my word.
I have not been a reviler of the king.
'I have not obstructed the water (of the Nile).
'I have not cut off the arm of the river.
I have not reviled the gods.
I have not acted fraudulently.
'I have not withheld the offerings of the temples.
I have not spoiled the shewbread of the gods.
'I have not robbed the dead of their funeral cakes.
'I have not taken the milk from the suckling.
'I have not killed sacred animals.
'I did not catch the sacred birds of the gods.
'I did not drive off the sacred cattle from their pasture.
'I have not falsified the measures of corn.
'I have not tampered with the scales.
'I have not blown out the sacred flame at its time.

'I did not impede the procession of the gods.
I am pure. I am pure. I am pure."

This confession is followed by another, in which the number of forty-two sins is more clearly brought out, and in which the plea for justification is based upon the assurance that the dead has not robbed nor envied any, that he was no eavesdropper, nor a dissembler or deceiver of the deaf, and that he used no incantations against the king, or his own father, or the god.

Then follows the weighing of his heart as described above. When the verdict is favorable and he has been cleared of any impurity, his heart is restored, and, after several other ordeals, he is ushered into the bright Elysian Fields (the fields of Alu) beyond the water. According to one version, the boatman of the nether world, Nu-Urru (called in the *Gilgames* epos *Ur nimu*, the prototype of Charon), ferries him over the deep lake or canal. According to another, probably a later one, he is carried across on the wings of the ibis-headed Thoth.[7] Henceforth, he enjoys the perennial life of the blessed under the shadow of the tree of life, or the sycamore of Nut, the goddess of the sky, a true Osiris. But woe to him if he turns out guilty! There stood in front of Osiris' throne, in the corner of the Hall of Judgment, the dreadful figure of Amam, "the Devourer," in the shape of a hippopotamus, eager, with its widely opened fangs, to seize upon the dead. Likewise are the forty-two judges, in case of his condemnation, ready to exhibit their vindictive justice in their

' Sayce, *l. c.*, p. 191.

former capacity of destroying demons. The "Book of the Dead," being chiefly used for the protection of the dead, seemingly avoids bringing out the punishments awaiting the guilty. It only implies the imminent "second death," as his heart is not restored to him, and his dismemberment follows. But, elsewhere the fiercest tortures awaiting him, such as burning by hot coals, and plunging into deep waters, or cutting of the body into pieces by sharp swords, are depicted.

We have here the very origin of the Inferno and Paradiso.

Though the chapter in question is a comparatively late production, its ethical spirit has found its expression in far older parts of the literature, showing that, behind all the superstitious practices of the Egyptians, there prevailed among the higher classes a morality which can only be compared with that of the Bible. However justified, then, the sneer and ridicule were, which Greek and Jewish writers cast upon "the worshipers of cats and oxen," we cannot withhold our admiration for their advanced state in morality as well as in literature and art.

But there is another point worth mentioning with reference to our subject: It was in Egypt that the Christian doctrine of the Trinity arose, which is the alpha and omega of the "Divine Comedy," and this was due to the great influence that the Osiris myth exerted upon the whole land. It is not necessary to dwell at length on the tale, which was ever more embellished, as it spread over wider areas, and according to which Osiris, the goodly man-god, met a cruel death at the hand of Set, the Evil One (formerly his brother, the consuming sun god), who cut his body into fourteen pieces, and scattered them to the winds. He left in Horus, the god of the morning sun, a son and avenger; while Isis, his consort—the type of a loving wife and mother—after having buried the fourteen parts of Osiris in fourteen different tombs, mourned him in common with her sister Nephthys, as did the women of Babylon and Canaan lament over Tammuz, or Adonis, in ever-repeated songs. It was the tragic end of the god, with its pathetic appeal, that gave rise also to the Christian Trinity, exactly as the picture of Isis and the child, Horus, found imitation in the first artistic representation of the Mother Goddess and her Divine Babe. Even the sycamore tree, on whose branches the phœnix perched and in which the heart of Osiris was believed to dwell to cause his resurrection at the winter solstice, is this very day spoken of in Christian folk-lore as the tree under which the Holy Family found rest during their flight into Egypt. On the other hand, the resurrection of Osiris out of the sycamore tree, taken to have been his spinal column, gave rise to the Jewish and Mohammedan belief in the revival of the dead by means of the spinal bone of resurrection, called Luz (the hazelnut tree). [8]

---

[8] See Sayce, *l. c.*, p. 207; Brugsch, "Religion and Mythologic der Alten Aegypter," p. 634, and Jewish Encyclopedia, art. "Luz."

CHAPTER III

HELL AND HEAVEN IN HINDU AND PERSIAN LITERATURE

A. *India*

That the Persian or Zoroastrian religion, with its sharp
contrast between the principles of good and evil, was
the main factor in shaping the eschatological views of
Judaism, Christianity, and Islamism is to-day generally
recognized. But the development of these views by
the Hindus, the Aryan kinsmen of the Persians, requires
our first consideration. For their well-nigh inexhaustible literary treasures, their hundreds of books of poetry,
philosophy, and law, now rendered for us into the Eng-
lish tongue, give us an insight into their endeavors to
unravel the mystery of the soul from the time when
they still lived in their ancient Aryan home to the period
of their higher civilization, when, within sight of India's
gigantic mountains and dazzling splendor of life, they
indulged more and more in fantastic concepts of things,
producing visions and legends concerning modes of
retribution after life, which anticipated and soon
eclipsed the Inferno and Purgatorio of Dante, and his
many predecessors. In fact, they imparted to Pythagoras and Plato, and indirectly to Christianity, that *other-*

worldly character, of which the "Divine Comedy" was the last great exponent. By nature of a cheerful and optimistic disposition, like the Greeks, they spoke of the soul's future destiny simply as of "the path the fathers walked." They looked up to their gods in heaven as ideal men, hoping to participate in their feasting and drinking on departing hence, as the Teuton warriors, when admitted to Valhalla, or the Greek heroes on Olympus. Next to Varuna (= Uranus), the mighty ruler of heaven, came Yama, the Persian Yima or Djemshid, whose spacious hall in the third heaven, brimful of light and joy, was the constant object of their praise in the songs of the Vedas. There, under a beautiful tree, surrounded by the gods and the fathers, he sat, quaffing the heavenly Soma sap, while streams of milk and honey were flowing in abundance round about. Sensual pleasures, including those of sex, prevailed. To the nether world they gave as yet little thought, though they occasionally consigned the liars, murderers, and wicked women to the dark abyss. At an early period, however, Yama was looked upon as the first man and, like the Persian Djemshid, as the ruler of men in the golden paradisiacal era, but soon he became also the first to enter the nether world, the leader and the stern judge of the dead. His two four-eyed dogs, one of whom bore the name of Çabala (= the Greek Cerberus), functioned as messengers of death and as guardians of the nether world, preventing the evildoers from entering the realm of bliss, situated beyond the river of death. Also, a recorder with an open book was placed at his side, and scales were there, as in Egypt, in which to weigh the sins of the dead.[1] (Soon the Brahmin imagination reveled in creating ever so many hells, with terrible forms of punishment for the guilty, one more appalling than the other. The original number of three—corresponding to the three heavens—grew to seven, then to twenty-one (in the Laws of Manu iv. 88), and further on to one hundred and thirty-six hells, and more. As the idea of just retribution demanded, in all ancient laws, exact retaliation, so was each crime, whether of a ritual or moral character, to be punished in the same form in which, and on the same part of the body with which, it was perpetrated by the living. As in Dante's Inferno, the eyes of the lustful or the envious are pulled out by the sharp beaks of birds; the tongue of the slanderer, blasphemer, and liar is hacked to pieces by pointed swords; the ear that listened with grim delight to malicious tales is plucked off by hot, iron spits; hands or feet employed in wrongdoing are put in seething caldrons; and these penalties are to be continued for a thousand years.—As to the heavenly reward for the virtuous, the writers are less prolific in their description. One feature we discern in these visions, which afterward recurs in Persian, Greek and medieval descriptions, and this is that the hero, a son or a favorite of the gods, or the saint, lapses into a comatose state, an apparent death, lasting for a number of days, during which the soul, freed from the body, was believed to enter the nether and upper worlds, to espy the secrets of the

---

[1] Zimmer, "Altindisches Leben," pp. 408-422; Oldenberg, "Die Religion der Veda," pp. 524-543.

hereafter, so as to be able to communicate them to those around. Among these there are some really beautiful and touching legends.[2] One tells of a virtuous king who had attained the bliss of the seventh heaven, but was, on account of some unkind act to one of his domestic animals, consigned to a gruesome hell, filled with mud, blood, and flames of fire, and with human victims of vulturelike birds, and there, as the sight of the numerous unfortunates who suffered the most terrible agonies, he forgot his own pain and woe, so that the very breath of his sympathetic soul brought relief to all to bring cheer to the beatified in Heaven as well as to himself. And this story of compassion and sympathy on the part of a king doomed to suffer for a while in hell, as atonement for some small shortcoming, was spun out in another more touching tale, reminding one of Christ's descent into Hell. Having been led by the servant of Yama, the judge, through the various apartments of hell, to learn of the relentless execution of justice, he hears, while on the point of leaving, the cry from all sides: "O stay with us, if but for a brief space of time, since thy presence assuages our agony!" Thereupon, thoroughly moved by this appeal, he resolves to renounce the heavenly bliss awaiting him for his good deeds and, instead, to derive a more intense happiness from redeeming those doomed to unbearable suffering. Thus he prevails upon Yama and Indra, the supreme god, to grant release to all the unfortunate. The legend reappears in part in the last book of

---

[2] See about all these Lucian Scherman's "Materialien zur Geschichte Indischen Visionsliteratur."

the Mahabharata, in connection with the death of its last hero, Yudhishithra, the son of Yama, who, on seeing his fellow heroes in hell instead of in heaven, is taught the lesson that, as no good deed even of the worst of men remains unrewarded, so must the slightest failing of the most virtuous be atoned for before their entrance into the realm of supreme bliss.

But there loomed up, in the Hindu mind, a view of the universe which proved fateful to its mode of thinking as well as to many thinkers in other lands—the doctrine of transmigration. Beholding in the whole of life a vast immensity, in which all diversity of beings, of gods, men, beasts, and plants, is undergoing a continuous transformation, passing from one state of life into the other in an endless cycle, a constantly revolving "wheel of destiny," they combined, by a strange theosophy, this concept with the idea of retribution, making the ascending and descending scale of beings dependent on the conduct of the souls in the various states of life —the *Karma*. Accordingly, those whose merit endows them with goodness—so the Law of Manu xii, 4, tells —reach the state of gods; those endowed with activity reach the state of men; whereas those endowed with darkness in their craving for sensual pleasures sink to the condition of beasts. Hence "the slayer of a Brahmin enters the womb of a dog, a pig or a jackal; he who steals . . . becomes a wolf, a bear, or a bird; and other violators enter the bodies of insects or the form of shrubs." Other writers picture the breaker of his word, the thief, the adulterer, and so forth, as passing into the forms of fish, worms, jackals, or ants. Reborn thus as men, they are tested anew, to determine whether they may regain a higher state of existence. Thus the whole of life appears to be a sort of purgatory, cleansing the soul from former impurity. Inasmuch, however, as the Karma, the merit or demerit inherent in the soul from a previous existence, threatens those who have risen to a higher state to be cast down again into a lower one, their lives are beset with fear and distress, so as to mar their bliss. There seemed but one way of escape from this endless woe of the cycle of existence for the Brahmin philosophy to offer, and this was to be thoroughly merged into the pantheistic All-soul, or All-breath, called Brahma, or Atman, with the full surrender of individuality.

Numerous saints resorted to hermit life, as did the naked philosophers, the Gymnosophists, who may have had influence on the Greek school of Cynics, or to systems of self-discipline culminating in self-torture, so as to become insensible to all pain and to make even the gods in heaven shudder at their superior miraculous power. They all took flights of thought to heights as bewildering and overawing, and also as isolating, as the Himalaya Mountains.

At last Buddha came to offer the panacea for all ills of life, in teaching the wise to surrender the will of thought, action, and purpose and enter the state of perfect passivity, the peace of *Nirvana*. In a world of universal suffering and disappointment, the royal beggar monk, in his pessimism——which so greatly appealed to Schopenhauer——demanded tender compassion and sympathy with all fellow creatures as the prerequisite step for the real solution of life's problem—spiritual self-extinction. Different from the Jewish and Christian systems of faith, hope, and love, embodied in Dante's "Divine Comedy," Buddha's world is a world deprived of purpose and divine foresight, a world without faith and hope. As the climate of India has become oppressive and enervating for its inhabitants, because it lacks the refreshing breezes of the sea, so was, seemingly, their mind impelled to revert to its own self, after having lost contact with the larger currents of humanity and its aims and activities. But the reaction came not only for the religion of Buddha, when the people reclaimed all the old gods and all the innumerable hells and heavens of old, but also for Buddha's life itself, which was made the object of endless transformations. The widely circulated stories about these, made India the land of wonders and fables for the Western world. Quite characteristic is the story told of the Chinese goddess, Kwan Yin, who refused to obey her father's command to marry and underwent a cruel death at his hand, whereupon a white tiger appeared and carried her body into a forest. There her disembodied spirit wanders through Yama's various hells, while she constantly invokes Buddha as "the Lord of Paradise," and behold, at her every step the horrors of hell disappear, and Yama finds his hells transformed into a paradise. "How shall men ever grow better, if there be no longer hell to chastise them?" cries forth the judge of the nether world, and he sends her back to the forest. There she awakens from her dream, finally, to learn that it was all Buddha's work, in whose service she now became a sister of mercy, helping to rescue the lives of mariners, and restoring even her cruel father from illness to health.

B. *Persia*

Ancient Persia cannot be compared with India as to her literature, which is as rich and varied in form and thought as is her luxuriant natural world. All the more prominent is Persia's place as a political and religious power in the history of nations. The founder of her great empire, the world-conqueror, Cyrus, is hailed by the great prophet of the Exile, the so-called Deutero-Isaiah, as "the Lord's anointed, called from the East to subdue the nations and loosen the loins of kings, to make the crooked places straight, and cut asunder the bars of iron, so as to make known from the rising of the sun unto the West that there is none beside Him, though he himself did not know Him who formed the light and created darkness, who maketh peace and createth evil, the Lord who doeth all these things." [3] Indeed, Cyrus inaugurated a reign of wisdom, tolerance, and freedom for the Eastern world not known before. In subjecting ancient Babylonia, and, afterward Egypt, to their rule, the whole royal ·dynasty did away with the cruel rites of idolatry, and led the people to a higher civilization. While adopting the cultural elements of the former kingdoms, they made the pursuit of virtue, truth and right the aim of their reign. Yet it was as worshipers of Ormazd, the supreme god, the god of

[3] Is. xlv, 1-7.

light and purity, the principle of good in the Zoroastrian system, whom they identified with Israel's "God of heaven," that they achieved their victories. It is not within our province here to expatiate on the Zoroastrian religion as laid down in the sacred books of the "Avesta," the product of many generations of priests who turned the simple faith or law of the reformer into a bewildering code of ritualism and dogmatism. Suffice it to say that, about a thousand years or more before the Christian era, Zoroaster appeared among the rugged toilers of the soil in Bactria, a land exposed to all the adversities of a rough climate and the hostile attacks of men and beasts, and as a prophet of Ormazd preached the lessons of thrift, purity, and law, while representing the whole of life as a constant combat against forces of evil. He beheld in the entire physical and moral world two diametrically opposed kingdoms, the kingdom of light, purity, and goodness under the dominion of Ormazd, the ruling intelligence, with his six beneficent forces or archangels, and the kingdom of darkness, impurity, and evil under the dominion of Ahriman, the principal of evil and destruction, with his six archfiends, and made battle on behalf of the former the very essence of religion. He thus gave the ancient Aryan religion a higher ethical character and purpose. Moreover, in contrast to the Hindu beliefs which ended in a philosophy of pessimism, he, or his successors, proclaimed, in a truly optimistic spirit, the final triumph of the principle of good, in announcing the downfall of Ahriman and his hosts at the end of the twelfth millennium of the world, the third millennium of the law of Zoroaster. Out of the seed of Zoroaster, miraculously preserved and conceived by a pure virgin, the world's savior (Soshiosh) will be born to make an end to the world of perdition, and amidst a great cataclysm, or conflagration, in which Ahriman and his serpent, the embodiment of falsehood and wrongdoing, will be consumed, he is to bring about the world of resurrection and of life eternal. Then the dead will rise to a new life, but they will have to undergo the great judgment at the bridge, Chinvad ("the bridge of judgment"), guarded by dogs, beneath which lies the deep abyss of hell, and beyond which is the road to Ormazd's heavenly "Abode of Song" (Garomana). The judgment is conducted by Ormazd's chief angel, Serosh, the personification of prayer, by Mithra, the genius of truth, and Rashnu, that of justice, who has, as in Egypt, charge of the scales wherein the soul is weighed. Those who prove to be good are met by a most beautiful maiden, who is the reflection of their own good life, and then led to the celestial paradise on top of Mount Alburz, whereas the wicked are met by a most ugly maiden, the reflection of their own wicked life, and then drop from the narrow bridge into hell to encounter its bitter torments. During the first three days after death, however, the demons and the angels fight for the possession of the soul, just as Satan and Michael, the archangel, fight for the Child of the Virgin in Revelation xii, 7 f., and for Moses in the Jewish Haggada; but the good souls also, during this time, have to pass the fire of purgatory, though without the pain which the bad ones suffer. Prayers and sacrifices for the dead, however, are of great benefit to all, we are told.

The Zoroastrian religion insists upon the threefold goodness of man, goodness in action, in thought, and in speech. Accordingly, the three heavens leading up to the topmost heaven, the abode of Ormazd and his six archangels, were designated to be the heaven of good action, the heaven of good thought, and the heaven of good speech. Through these the good are to be successively led up by Vohuman, the keeper of Paradise, to the "Abode of Song," the seat of the uncreated light! There they are given the food of immortality, consisting of the marrow of the primeval ox, slain by Soshiosh (the savior) and his helpers in the work of resurrection, fifteen men and women of the immortals, and likewise the drink of immortality, prepared out of the heavenly Soma from the tree of life. Obviously we have here something similar to the Greek ambrosia and nectar of the Olympian gods. Corresponding to the three heavens leading up to the mansion of bliss, there are also three hells, one of bad action, another one of bad thought, and a third one of bad speech, leading down to the abode of utter darkness and woe, the habitation of Ahriman and his host of demons, where the wicked are fed on poisonous filth. As to those whose good and evil deeds are about equal, they are consigned to a neutral place to remain "ever stationary," until their future destiny is decided.

It is easy to see that this artificial system is the work of long growth and development, as the Parsee literature plainly shows, and undoubtedly both Semitic and Hindu elements helped in shaping it. This is especially indicated by the remarkable vision of heaven and hell described by Arda Viraf, the Wise, frequently referred to in Parsee writings, and apparently modeled after Hindu legends, but, at the same time, following older descriptions, which gave rise to similar apocalyptic visions, both Jewish and Christian, if not also Grecian ones. It is especially interesting to find here an exact prototype of Dante's Inferno and Paradiso. Arda Viraf—thus runs the story—was chosen by his fellow priests as the best and wisest, to serve as medium for the ascertaining of the mysteries of the hereafter, and was given a sleeping potion to fall into a comatose state for seven days, during which time his soul would leave his body and wander through heaven and hell. There, at the Chinvad bridge, he sees first, precisely as does Dante in his Inferno, those "undecided," who, from lack of merit, are kept there, unable to pass, and exposed to suffering from the constant interchange of heat and cold. Then he mounts up to the three heavens, first to the one inhabited by the men of good action, but devoid of ceremonial observations, the sphere of the stars; after this, to the second heaven, the sphere of the moon; and hence, to the third heaven, the sphere of the sun, where he recognizes those who had been beneficent rulers on earth. But here the description deviates from the old system, having seven instead of four heavens. At the fourth, his guide, Serosh, offers him the bread of immortality which, like the Greek Lethe, makes the soul forget all bodily experience and, at the same time, enables it to gaze without fear at all the splendor of heaven. Further up, he beholds the souls of tillers of the soil and of shepherds who have been faithful followers of the law, in the midst of beautiful gardens, replete with rarest flowers, and clad in gold- and silver-woven garments, with diadems on their heads, attended by most attractive maidens, all earning their reward for having been kind to the poor and, likewise, to their domestic animals. Finally, on reaching the seventh heaven, the abode of the eternal light, he is dazed by the grandeur and splendor surrounding him, and in the midst of this celestial Paradise he beholds Zoroaster on a throne, surrounded by the heroes and kings of the past, of the Golden Age. Strange to say, like Dante, during his stay in Paradise, he is initiated into the whole theological system which he is to promulgate.

All the more awful and overwhelmingly sad is the sight he encounters upon entering hell, with its pestilential vapors, and its putrid waters, in which the unfortunates are tossed about without rest, amidst cries of woe to which the heavens seem deaf. One stream, presenting a most terrible aspect by its all-overpowering whirlpools, is—he is told—formed of the tears of those who incessantly lament over the dead they have lost, failing to submit to the decree of divine justice.

The punishments meted out to the sinners are similar to those described in the Hindu versions and in Dante's Inferno, in accordance with the principle of "Measure for Measure!" The former rich man who withheld his goods from the poor suffers unbearable thirst, and gnaws at his own flesh from hunger. The quarrelsome woman with the bad tongue is suspended with her head downward and her tongue twisted, and, likewise, the liar and blasphemer. Thus the whole catalogue of sins and crimes is passed muster, showing how each wrongdoer is repaid for his acts. One great sinner suffered unending torments in his whole body, only one foot remained untouched by the fire and the serpents. On noticing this, Arda Viraf asked his guide for the reason, and was told that once in his life the man showed pity upon a starving animal, and pushed some fodder toward it with this one foot of his, and this was his compensation. At the bridge of judgment another fearful sight struck the saint. One soul was fleeing full of terror from a pursuing demon, whose ghastly appearance made it shudder and cry in despair, but it was all in vain. The demon took hold of it and said: "Wilt thou not recognize me? I am thy own self. Thy own crimes have made me the ugly creature thou seest before thee. Instead of following the path of supporting the needy and leading others to the path of virtue, thou didst only evil things during thy life, and led others on the path of vice." And speaking thus, he seized the soul and cast it from the narrow bridge down into the abysmal depth of hell.

Surely, it is the language of humanity that is spoken here in these "Sacred Books of the East." [4] The distant lands and the distant ages, with all their diversity of

[4] Max Mueller's "Sacred Books of the East," iv Zend Avesta i. pp. 212-218; Bundahis xxx, 120-144; xviii, p. 46 f; The Book of Arda Viraf, transl. by Haug, London, 1872, Spiegel, "Eranische Alterthamskunde," ii, 158 ff; Tiele's "Persian Religion"; Wm. Geiger "Ostiranische Cultur," pp. 272-286; Windischman, "Zoroastrische Studien"; Rawlinson, "Ancient Monarchies" ii, p. 337 ff.

form and of thought, seem to beckon us to listen to the one great symphony of religious aspiration and ethical idealism, and to say to us: *"Introite, et hic dii sunt—* "Enter, for here, too, dwells the Deity that lives in all those made in the image of God."

CHAPTER IV

A. *Greece*

As in our survey we approach the classic land of
Hellas, with its azure sky, its genial atmosphere, and its
hospitable shore offering an extensive view of the
Asiatic coast opposite and the many islands studded
about like sparkling precious stones upon the Ægean
sea, we feel as if nature had here done its utmost to
prepare the soil for a race superior to the rest in body
and mind. Indeed, the Hellenic race, being of a finer
build and a brighter mind, richer in imaginative power,
enterprise, and skill than the average population elsewhere, was, by its geographical and historical position,
destined to take over the best elements of a culture
attained by the process of thousands of years before,
and cast them into a new mold that was to bear the
stamp of a higher European civilization. Here was
to be cradled a new type of humanity. In their proud
self-consciousness the Greeks looked upon the rest of
mankind as barbarians, forgetful of the fact that it
was, in the main, owing to their rare power of assimi-
lation that they were enabled to achieve the great task
assigned to them in history. Only by following in the

van of the seafaring Phœnicians who, centuries before, had settled all along the Ægean coast and on the islands around, they acquired the skill of navigation and commerce together with the art of writing, adopting from them even the very names of the instruments and products they used. From the Persians and Assyrians they learned, through the mediatorship of the Phrygians and Lydians, how to create works of art, and recent discoveries have put us on the trail of the culture of Crete and other centers of a remote civilization, to which they were indebted for their beginnings of cultural life. On the formation of their religious concepts also, apart from their Indo-European traditions, the ancient Semitic races exerted a prominent influence, and their gods and heroes found easy admission into the Greek pantheon. Who, for instance, would recognize in Aphrodite, "the foam-born" goddess of beauty and love, the vulgar Phœnician Asthoreth of Cyprus, the goddess of fertility, or in Poseidon, the Sidonian god of the sea? Or in Hermes the Egyptian Thoth, and in the Minotaur of Crete, the blood-thirsty Moloch, and so many other foreign gods and goddesses in their attractive Hellenic guise? Thus the Greek "Elysian fields" (Elysium) are none other than the Egyptian "fields of Alu," just as Rhadaman-thys, who dwells there, has been shown by Naville and Zuendel, the Egyptologists, to be the Grecized Rha d Amenti ($=$ the ruler of the nether world). The fact is, the Greek genius was endowed with the wondrous power of recasting the figures and concepts borrowed from others into forms and characters of its own. Like Midas' hand, it turned all it touched into the gold of artistic beauty and lucid thought. Its aim and object was not, like that of other nations and empires, either conquest or exploitation of lands, but solely the unfolding of all human faculties, to attain the highest standard of culture, of esthetic and intellectual valor and dignity. Accordingly, poets, painters, sculptors, and writers vied with each other in representing their Olympian gods and goddesses as idealized men and women, whether in power or stature, in symmetry or harmony of form, beautiful and impressive reflections of their own individuality, but with all human frailty and passion, and as anything but exemplars of morality. Different from the Hebrews, who beheld in man the creature made in the likeness of God, they made their gods in the likeness of man, thus elevating them above the level of blind and crude nature, but at the same time viewing humanity as the end and acme of life. The Greeks thus became the unequaled masters of art and literature for all time, the teachers of philosophy and the pathfinders of science, the fashioners of our whole civilization.

And yet, with all their surpassing gifts and aspirations, which make us look up with admiration and gratitude to the genius of a Homer and a Phidias, a Plato and an Aristotle in whose footsteps we are still walking, they themselves at last felt one great gap in their make-up. They lacked the upward look to "a Power not ourselves that maketh for righteousness," for love and holiness. It has well been said that the word holiness, in our sense, was not in their vocabulary. They had no sacred books, nor prophets, to bring them the message of hope and courage from a higher world,

and invest their ethics with the authority and power of
a divine imperative. Their wise men, their first
philosophers—whether materialists, like Heraclitus, or
idealists, like Xenophanes—turned away with haughty
disdain, as did their sophists and comic writers with
scorn and ridicule, from the gods worshiped by the
masses, slaves of their passions and whims like themselves. But having outgrown their Olympian deities,
they failed to lift the godhead within to the heights of
a sublime ethical ideal, as did the Hebrew prophets.
However grand were the efforts of their great tragic
poets, Æschylus and Sophocles, to represent the heroes
of the past as imposing types and mirrors of heaven-
aspiring humanity, their views of human destiny were,
after all, pathetic and melancholy, as they culminated
in a resigned submission to inexorable fate, to which
men and gods were alike subject. So does their lofty-
minded lyric poet, Pindar, endeavor in vain to remove
the stains of moral impurity from the old deities, and,
with his hero worship and belief in transmigration of
souls, he still remains on polytheistic ground. Socrates,
the preacher to the men on the street, with his high
ideals, surely awakened, to a certain degree, the God-
consciousness in his contemporaries, and his dissent
from the crowd brought the martyr's death upon him.
More positive and clear was his great pupil, Plato, the
poet philosopher, in pointing to a divine goodness holding sway over a world of ideas, or heavenly images,
in which the world below was mirrored, to emulate
which was to be man's highest aim; and yet his God,
having another subaltern god to do the work of creation

for him, lacked the liberty and super-mundane power of the absolute Being of monotheism. Consequently the human soul, imprisoned in the body, had none to open its prison door for true freedom and a larger outlook of life. Neither he nor his great disciple, Aristotle, the comprehensive master mind of knowledge, who beheld above the ever-revolving world spheres an all-moving Intelligence in continuous action yet devoid of self-conscious purpose, gave the people what they essentially craved for, a religion to offer them the bread of life for their hungry soul. What followed these leaders of thought in the various schools was merely a compromise or an expression of despair on the part of some, but no solution of life's problem. Hence the serious-minded resorted to the mysteries of cults introduced from without, under the name of the frantic Thracian god, Dionysius, or of Orpheus, the mystic bard of obscure origin. As a matter of fact, India and Egypt, under these hidden names, had to unfathom for the initiated the secrets of the hereafter, and tell them of the souls' state and the readjustment in another world of life's inadequacies here, exactly as, in our days, those that have lost their moorings in the accepted forms of religion seek refuge for their bewildered soul in spiritualism and kindred systems. And this brings us to our main theme, the eschatological literature of the Greeks.[1]

The Homeric Hades (literally "the Unseen," the ruler and then the realm of the nether world) is, as

---

[1] Tiele, "Outlines of the History of Religion," p. 201ff; Hasting's Encyclopedia of Religion and Ethics, art. "The Greeks."

has been stated above, like Sheol, the dark abode of the shades in the depths of the earth, with its entrance at the extreme Western ends, where the ocean flows. It is guarded by the three-headed dog Cerberus, originally, as in Babylonia, a devouring demon, but later on represented as friendly to the newcomers, but a fierce assailant of those attempting to escape. Charon, the ferryman who received the obolus coin from each entering the gloomy realm (as a peace offering from the survivors), was, likewise, originally, as he appeared in old Etruscan pictures and in modern Greek folklore, the demon of death. Hermes, the god of the winds, became, like the Egyptian Thoth, the conductor of souls. Now the eleventh book of the Odyssey, which was taken by Vergil as his model for the "Æneid," presents by no means, as does the latter, the descent of the hero into the infernal regions to meet the departed. Instead of this, the hero, following the advice of Circe, desires to learn from Tiresias, the famous seer transferred to the nether world, the outcome of his trying voyage from land to land. Standing on the shore of the Western ocean at the entrance to Hades, he offers to the shade of the seer and others sacrificial blood, to give them the semblance of life, and he summons them to himself rather than wander across the rivers of death in search of them. From where he stands he sees his mother, his friends, and his kinsmen, the heroes and heroines of the Trojan War, and likewise the Cretan Minos, the judge, Orion, the huntsman, and Hercules, with his bow, in their former occupations, and finally the three noted penitents, Tityus, Tantalus, and Sisyphus, as they suffered in the upper world for their offenses against the gods. A retribution of the deeds of mortals in Hades was not at all intended by the poet, who does not even refer here to the Elysium spoken of elsewhere in the Odyssey (iv. 560 ff.) as

> "the blissful plains
> Of the utmost earth where Rhadamanthys reigns,
> Where joys ever young, mixed with pain or fear,
> Fill the wide circle of the eternal year,
> Where from the breezy deep the blessed inhale
> The fragrant murmur of the Western gale. . . ."

And these were "afforded them by the gods as a peculiar grace," but not as the place of reward for good deeds.

The idea of retribution in after life was first brought home to the people by the Eleusinian mysteries, in which the descent into Hades of Demeter, the goddess of the earth, in quest of Persephone, her daughter, dramatized in symbolic form the going down of the seed into the soil to reappear in the new garb of grain in spring, thereby to express the idea of man's entering death in order to rise to a new life thereafter. While at first offering the promise of bliss only to the initiated, these mysteries afterward took a wider scope, and gave rise to a division of the souls in Hades into the morally pure and therefore blessed, and the morally impure and therefore doomed to suffer. But it was chiefly due to the Orphic mysteries, in which only a select aristocratic class participated, that the idea of an after-life retribution was developed and systematically elaborated.

It is difficult to say how far the ecstatic state called

forth by the wild Dionysian cult produced the vision of the soul's defying all limitations of space and time in its wanderings through hell and heaven, such as were ascribed to the mythical Orpheus and his followers, and worked out in numerous poems under his name. Already at an early period, we read of saints and heroes as having left their bodies to wander about from land to land.[2] An unbiased study of the subject seems to show that the train of ideas which influenced alike the Orphic brotherhood and the half religious, half philosophical order founded by Pythagoras in South Italy in the middle of the sixth century came, not from the barbarous people of Thrace, but from India and surrounding lands. Only there the belief in the transmigration or rebirth of the soul as a mode of purging it from former sins in an endless "wheel of existence" had taken deep root long before the Greeks knew of it, and it is exceedingly improbable that this strange doctrine should have risen in different countries independently of each other.

As to Orpheus, there can be little doubt that before he became the wondrous musician whose magic art tamed the wild beasts into silence, he was, like Osiris and Yama, a god of the nether world, as was his wife, Eurydice, the corresponding earth or hell goddess. He was even spoken of, like these, as the first man to die and enter there. Henceforth, his descent into Hades became the favorite theme of poetic and artistic representations. Greek mythology and Egyptian concepts helped in the working out of the system. The three

2 Rhode, "Psyche"; Albert Dieterich, "Nekyia."

Homeric penitents were made types of vices punished in Hades, the one of unbridled lust, the other of overbearing pride, and the third of insatiable greed. To these were added Ixion, as a type of deceit and treachery, and the Danaides pouring water into a sieve, as types of futile ambition. So were the Furies, as the avengers of wrongdoing, transferred from earth to Hades, while Elysium became the realm of bliss awaiting the pure and good. It was thus a deepened religious sense which made the better class look to the hereafter, to compensate for the shortcomings of this life. In other words, individualism, which had no real place either in the religion or in the philosophy of the Greeks, made itself felt more and more as a demand of the soul. And this became the dominant motive power and an almost religious force in the teaching of Pythagoras, whose followers are called theologians by Aristotle. We know too little of this extraordinary personality who started new movements in philosophy and particularly in science, whose studies comprised the spheres of the stars and the harmonies of music, and who was deeply concerned with the calculation of mathematics and the mystic significance of numbers—a great teacher of ethics and a devout seeker after God as "the One among the many," the center of the cosmic unity and harmony, "Whom man is to follow, striving like Him after harmony." Herodotus tells us that he owed his knowledge to Egypt; modern investigators, with far better reason, find him to have been an adept of Hindu lore.[3] His

---

[3] L. Schroeder, "Pythagoras u. d. Inder"; Encyclopedia of Religion and Ethics, art. "Pythagoras and the Pythagoreans."

system was centered upon his belief in the transmigration of the soul, the constant undergoing of the process of rebirth in human and animal form, while at the same time meeting retribution of its deeds in Hades, exactly as the various Hindu visions have it. But he connected it all with the cult of the Greek gods of the nether world and, especially, with that of Apollo of Delphi. He left no written work of his own, though descriptions of a descent to Hades were ascribed to him as well as to his followers. It was even said of him, as of Buddha, that he recalled the memory of his former existence; moreover, that, once, when he passed a howling dog who had been beaten, he stopped it, saying that he recognized in him a former friend. Whatever such legends may amount to, it is certain that he strove to make his life and his outer appearance the embodiment of perfect purity as he taught it, and his abstinence from meat seems to have been based on his transmigration theory. Recent discoveries of hundreds of little gold plates belonging to the fourth and fifth pre-Christian centuries, which contain extracts of the Pythagorean system of belief in after-life retribution, and which have apparently been deposited as charms for the dead in those tombs or coffins of South Italy (and also of Crete), like the Osirian formulas in Egypt, have shown the large extent of the Pythagorean propaganda, and verified the claims of the order.

It is interesting to notice that, instead of drinking from the water of Lethe (= Oblivion), the soul was here told to drink from the water of Mnemosyne (= Remembrance) on the right side of the road in order to rise to a higher state, whereas the Lethe water on the left side was to be avoided—a distinction which we frequently meet henceforth. Alongside of the two classes of souls, the wicked and the faithful, we find mentioned here, for the first time, a middle class, as in the Parsee system, whose fate remains in suspense for a thousand years (= one æon), or more, until they are allowed to walk upward on "the road to Zeus." Pindar, in one of his odes, speaks of a threefold purgation, and elsewhere of nine (= 3×3) years. Empedocles, regarded like Pythagoras, his master, as a priest and prophet of the order, declares that one guilty of murder or perjury has for thirty thousand seasons (that is for ten thousand years) to pass through the various forms of life until his crime is atoned for.

The best informed writer on these Orphic and Pythagorean mysteries is Plato. In the form of mystic allegory, he tells first in his "Phædrus" (§ 247 f.), of the joyous life of the gods in heaven, whose divine intelligence feeds their souls—amidst the revolution of the worlds—on truth, on absolute justice, temperance, and knowledge which "give them ambrosia to eat and nectar to drink." The human souls, on the other hand, are either carried by their charioteers or wings upward to the realm of truth or downward to the earth, and by the law of retribution, the one becomes a philosopher or an artist, the other a righteous king, the third a politician, the fourth a physician, the fifth a prophet or hierophant, the sixth a poet, the seventh a husbandman, the eighth a demagogue, and the ninth a tyrant. These remain in a state of probation for ten thousand years

(= ten æons). At the end of three æons the guileless philosopher has passed this state and enters the divine life; the others have to enter "the House of Correction" under the earth, before they choose their second life. Then they, according to their merit, pass into the life of a beast and then again to that of man, whereas some will not pass into human forms any more. The philosopher, who will cling to the recollection of the things he saw when in company with God, will remain blessed, having been initiated into the sacred mysteries.

Less mystical is Plato in his "Republic" (§ 614 ff). There he at once tells of the vision of Er, a Pamphylian warrior, who, exactly like the Persian saint, Arda Viraf, left his body on the twelfth day of his death and beheld two chasms in the earth corresponding to two others in heaven. In the intermediate space there sat judges bidding the just to ascend on the right side to heaven with marks on their foreheads, and commanding the unjust, with marks on their backs, to descend on the left to the lower regions. The former ones went forth into the meadow of bliss, while recalling their sufferings on earth during a thousand years' journey; for they had to suffer *tenfold* for every wrong done during their hundred years of earthly life. So were also the rewards of beneficence and justice *tenfold*. Mention is made also of infants who died too early for judgment. We have here, already, the Limbus Infantium. Especially terrible were the punishments inflicted upon such as committed sins of impiety against gods and parents, or upon murderers, suicides, and tyrants, but always commensurate with their crimes, as were also the rewards of the just. He then dwells at length on the bright light, like the color of the rainbow, which he saw in midheaven where the spindle of Necessity is revolving, moving amidst the music of hymning sirens, the seven planetary spheres. In the sphere above, where perfect harmony reigns, the three Fates, the daughters of Necessity, hold forth the lots to the mortals for the new life, saying: "Virtue is free, and as man honors or dishonors her, he will have more or less of her. The chooser is answerable; God is justified." Owing, however, to former existences, too many choose the life of animals instead of men. At the "river of Forgetfulness" they await the new life, into which they enter, amidst thunderstorm and earthquake, like shooting stars, accompanied by the genius they have chosen for their guardian.

In "Gorgias" (§ 525 f.) Plato devotes a chapter to the mode of judgment of the dead as arranged by Zeus, who appointed his three sons, Minos and Rhadamanthys from Asia, and Æakus from Europe, as judges to be placed at the three roads, of which two lead to the Isles of the Blessed and the third to Tartarus. In his "Phædo" (§ 113a) Plato speaks of the four streams of Hades, but differently from other writers, he mentions first the ocean flowing around the earth, then the Acheron flowing into the Acherusian Lake, next the "fiery" Periphlegeton, and finally the black river Styx, which he somehow identifies with Cocytus, the "howling" river. On the Acheron judgment is held, and those who have passed "a middle kind of life" are undergoing purification, being punished for their evildoings and rewarded for their good deeds. Then there are the incurable ones. Such as have committed great sacrileges or foul murders are hurled into Tartarus, never to come forth again. Those who are guilty of great, yet not unpardonable crimes—who, for instance, have in a moment of anger done violence to a father or mother, or taken the life of another, but have repented for the remainder of their life—are to undergo sufferings for a year, and then are cast forth, the homicides through the Cocytus and the parenticides through the Periphlegeton, into the Acherusian Lake, where they must stay until they have obtained pardon from those whom they have wronged. But those that have led a holy life are released from their earthly prison and go forth to the upper "mansions of bliss." Concerning these Plato, in the "Republic" (§ 363), says, with reference to Musæus and his son Orpheus, that "the saints are feasting on couches with crowns on their heads, passing their whole time in drinking," but somewhat satirically he adds that "the immortality of drunkenness can not be the highest meed of virtue."

All these descriptions, however colored by his own philosophy, evidence the prominence given by Plato to these mysteries, and his quotation from the vision of Er, the Pamphylian, leaves us in no doubt as to their Oriental origin. At the same time, the comic allusions to them by Aristophanes in his "Frogs," and by Lucian, the satirist, betray the unfavorable attitude of many toward these so-called sacred mysteries. Still they continued to furnish ever new material for poetic or prose compositions of such visions. To a number of these,

Plutarch, the prolific and eclectic writer of the first Christian century, refers, besides quoting Pindar and Plato as his authority. So in his "Dream of Socrates" Timarchos relates of his descent into the cave of Trophonius from where, after a two nights' and a day's stay, he wandered down to hell. There, amidst the howling of beasts and the groaning of men and children he walked through its four divisions to behold the stars, the sun, and the moon above, influencing the rise or fall of the souls. More similar to the descriptions given above is one told in the chapter on the Delay of Divine Punishment. There, the divine Aridæus tells how he, three days after a fatal fall from a precipice, found himself flung into mid-air between the high stars above and the deep, dark hell beneath, where he recognized some friends among the fluttering souls. The three Furies, the daughters of Necessity, held judgment, as in Plato, decreeing three kinds of punishment, according to the manner of the crime committed, while each soul showed by its color whether cruel murder, or lasciviousness or envy was the ruling passion of its life. Besides notorious malefactors, hypocrites had to undergo severe punishment. Slanderers were twisted together, gnawing at each other's flesh. Three kinds of lakes were there, one of boiling gold, another of chilling lead, and a third of rugged iron, while demons whetted their instruments for the punishment of these different classes of sinners. Among the wailings of the unfortunate he heard the voice of his own father calling him, and confessing that he had poisoned his guests for the sake of the gold they had, but he dared not interfere.

On the opposite side he came to a very spacious palace, radiant with light and fragrant with the perfume of all sorts of flowers. There the souls, flocking in like birds, were banqueting amidst sounds of joy and laughter. This was the abode of Bacchus (= Dionysius) and called the place of Lethe (= oblivion). It had a rarified air. Goblets of many colors were seen, and the voice of Sibyl, the prophetess, was heard. But the last scene he saw was the preparation of the souls for the second life awaiting them, a kind of purgatory. He was also shown the Crater where Orpheus found the soul of his wife, Eurydice.

With many of these visions Vergil was undoubtedly familiar. Not so Dante, who probably knew no Greek.

B. *Rome*

Of Roman literature little need be said here. Much as was achieved by the Romans in the field of law and statecraft, in literature in general they lacked originality. They were simply imitators of the Greeks. Whatever peculiarity their religion possessed, in which abstract ideas, as in Parseeism, prevailed, they admitted at a later period the Greek deities, one after the other, into their Pantheon, borrowing the grace and grandeur from Olympian deities with which they identified their own.[4] As they extended their empire over the East, they accorded also to the Asiatic and Egyptian goddesses a place in their Pantheon. What a prominent place the Cumæn Sibyl played in their early history is well known.

[4] See Tiele, *l. c.,* p. 228 f.

As to the visionary literature, it was Cicero, the skillful popularizer of Hellenic thought, who offers in his "Dream of Scipio" a fair reproduction of the Greek vision of Hades. But Vergil's "Æneid" occupies a place of its own alongside of Homer's "Odyssey." Æneas' visit to Hades is, in fact, a great improvement upon that of Odysseus', owing to Vergil's acquaintance with Plato and the Orphics. The poem is above all prompted by a higher design, being permeated by a certain moral purpose. The uncanny Homeric Circe is replaced by the Cumæan Sibyl, who by her wisdom directs the hero's wanderings through the gloomy "house of Proserpina" where law and order hold sway, and to which also Charon, the dreadful ferryman with his boat ever freighted anew with souls, and grim Cerberus, the hellhound lurking at the river Styx, own allegiance. After having bestowed the much-coveted funeral rites upon the wretched unburied, which was also Odysseus' first act of piety, Æneas encounters, before crossing the Acheron River, first, newborn babes torn from their mothers, thus realizing not so much the horrors of hell as the bitterness of death. Then his human pity is roused by the sight of those whom judicial error has sadly robbed of their young life. Next to these he finds at "the mournful fields" a group of suicides lamenting over their rash deed prompted by disappointed and unrequited love. Finally, his woe is mixed with pride, as he meets his heroic kinsmen who have fallen as victims of the Trojan War. On reaching the interior of hell he comes to the parting of the roads, where the path on the right leads to "Pluto's golden palace," while the left leads down to the dismal depth of Tartarus. Overlooking the wide realm on the left, he sees treble walls, surrounded by the fiery Phlegeton River, enclosing the towers of Tartarus, where the groans of the tormented rent the air. There Rhadamanthys holds stern judgment, inquiring into the manner, place, and time of each crime committed during lifetime, before passing the rigid sentence, while the Furies stand hard by, eager to execute the sentence with the aid of the horrible monsters at their command. In the meanwhile the dire warning is echoed forth by their fierce messenger, Phlegyas, "Learn righteousness, and dread the avenging deities!" The Titan race comes first to sight, terrific examples of the unrelenting wrath of the offended gods; then follow the tyrants, the traitors, those guilty of incest and murder, all paying their penalty for the crimes perpetrated.

Turning to the right, Æneas, immersed with Lethe's rejuvenating water, enters the verdant fields of bliss, where the happy souls listen to Orpheus' harmonious notes, themselves joining in the song, some exercising their limbs in sport, others feasting. Finally meeting his long-sought-for father, Anchises, he learns all about the destiny of the human soul. He is told of the mysterious "wheel" of constant rebirth. For a thousand years the souls have to undergo the punishments and penances that are to cleanse them from stains clinging to them from bygone existences. "Some are hung to bleach in the wind, others are plunged in water, and again others purged in fire. They all prepare for 'the second life.' And yet, only the few will breathe the soft Elysian air to enjoy happiness in the pure ether of the soul, after they have tasted of the Lethean flood to sweep the memory of past labors and cares beyond recall."

It is the transmigration theory of Plato and the Orphics that Vergil embodied in his poem, which ends with the hopeful outlook upon imperial Rome, founded by the descendants of Æneas. Of course, Dante's Catholic faith bade him discard the transmigration idea. Instead, his regeneration of the soul is effected by the stages of the purgatory. On the further development of the concept of the Inferno and Purgatorio the following chapters will cast new light.

CHAPTER V

The general impression is that the "Apocrypha,"
which belong to the period intervening between the Old
and the New Testaments, and are placed in our larger
Bible editions between these two, form the connecting
link between them. But this is erroneous. Though the
"Book of Wisdom" and the second "Book of the Maccabees" contain views pointing to a new religious concept of life, the "Apocrypha," on the whole, did not
exert a decisive influence on either the Synagogue or
the Church. Quite different is the place occupied by
the apocalyptic literature. The writings which appeared under the assumed name of older biblical sages
—therefore, also called the "Pseudepigrapha"—during
the two centuries preceding the Christian era and the
two following centuries,—having for their purpose the
revealing "of the hidden events of the future"; or of
the mysteries of "the things to happen at the end of
time,"—wrought a perceptible change of thought in the
minds of the people. They led to a new world view,
widely differing from the ancient Israelitish one, and

they actually interlink the Old and the New Testaments. Reinterpreting and thus reëchoing the old prophecies, the apocalyptic writers and speakers claimed to be possessed of the Divine Spirit, like the prophets of yore, while announcing the advent of the longed-for Messianic era with its preceding day of doom, the Day of God's primitive wrath, for heathenism, and at the same time offering new hope for the people chafing under the yoke of Syrian or Roman oppression. Nor was theirs a mere national hope or a message confined to Judea, as was in the main that of the older prophecies, but it bore a more universal character, voiced, as it was, as a long-hidden "secret" of heaven. Since the great expectations of Israel's rejuvenation, roused by the exilic and post-exilic seers, were not realized, these apocalyptic seers boldly declared that "the end of days" was nigh, and a regeneration of the whole universe was to follow, in which the heathen kingdoms, together with all the God-defying hosts of heaven and earth, would be swept away, and death itself be swallowed up forever. However much these Apocalyptists were indebted for such radical world concepts to Parseeism, they gave their message its specific Jewish character by their preaching of righteousness, by their stern insistence on repentance, by their revival of the prophetic appeal: "Wash you, make you clean; put away the evil of your doings; cease to do evil, learn to do well; seek justice, relieve the oppressed, and so forth" (Is. i, 16-17). Then, they promised, Israel would be compensated for all its sufferings, and its dead would rise from the grave to participate in the new life of the nation.

But what lent especial force and authority to these predictions was that they did not present them as emanating from their own minds, but as matters decreed from the beginning of the world, as cosmic mysteries that had come down from the wise men of the hoary past and been transmitted only to the few elect. As a matter of fact, these very ideas formed, as a closer study of Babylonian literature has shown us, part of the old Oriental wisdom, and offered mystic glimpses of a larger cosmos to widen their mental horizon.

But the Synagogue at large with its Scribes, the Pharisean doctors of the Law, could not afford to recognize these outpourings of the spirit as genuine prophecy, since for them the prophetic period closed with Malachi (Tos. Sota xiii, 2; I Macc. iv, 46; ix, 27 comp. Ps. lxxiv, 9). The very claim of secret lore was discountenanced for them by the Deuteronomic declaration: "The secret things belong unto the Lord our God" (Deut. xxix, 28 comp. Ben Sira iii, 22; Hagigah ii, 1). Only the saintly mystics, known by the name of *Essenes*, "the men of silence," or "the discreet ones," described by Philo and Josephus as living apart from the crowds and leading a holier life than even the Pharisean schoolmen, were the real keepers of the secret lore and the authors of the apocalyptic literature. The very woe and distress of the time, which made the people in their despondency cry out with the Psalmist (lxxiv, 9-10), "How long, how long, O God, shall the adversary reproach?" became to them the evidence of the approaching end, of the nearing crisis, which is to bring about the great Day of Judgment and the Messianic kingdom of God with its resurrection or regeneration of the world. Moreover, claiming to be initiated into the innermost plan of God's reign, they gave a survey of the world's history, pointing out the very time when the end was bound to come.

Now the "Book of Daniel" formed an exception among the Apocalyptic books, in being admitted into the collection of Holy Writings—though not, as was later done by the Church, among the prophetic books. The reason was that this Hasidean product had essentially helped in bringing about the Maccabean victory by the vision announcing the imminent overthrow of the reign of Antiochus, the Syrian king, and his hosts, by the miraculous intercession of God. Daniel, mentioned by Ezekiel, alongside of Noah and Job, as a righteous man and also as eminent by his great wisdom (Ezek. xiv, 14-20 and xxviii, 3), had apparently become a popular hero in Jewish folklore—and was aptly depicted by the Hasidean author as a typical saint whose staunch loyalty to his faith, despite threatening peril, served as an inspiring example to the people, and whose miraculous powers, which forced even the cruel tyrant to pay homage to God, could only render his wondrous visions all the more impressive.

Being the first work of its kind, it naturally became the model for the entire subsequent apocalyptic literature. There is, first of all, the artificial construction of Israel's history, based on Jeremiah's seventy years and rendered into seventy year-weeks (Dan. ix, 29 f.; comp. Jer. xxv, 11; xxix, 10), and likewise of the world's history, taking the four great world kingdoms, Babylonia,

Media, Persia, and Syria, symbolized by the four metals (ii, 35 f.) and the four beasts (vii, 4 ff.), as destined, by their successive downfall, to lead to the final appearance of the kingdom of God's holy ones, of Israel symbolized by the Son of Man in the clouds, which would last forever. The very "time of trouble such as never was, since there was any nation even to that same time," is declared as marking the great catastrophe when the final defeat will be brought upon the Adversary in heaven by the archangel, Michael. In the meantime the altar of God was to be polluted for three and a half years by the Syrian idol, Baal Shamem, called "the Abomination of Desolation." Then the people inscribed in God's book for life would be delivered. After this, "Many that sleep in the dust shall awake, some—the righteous or martyrs—to life everlasting, the others—the wicked—to everlasting shame and abhorrence" (xii, 1-4).[1]

Alongside of Daniel, *Enoch*, the grandfather of Noah, was selected as a typical saint by the apocalyptic writers. He seemed to be best fitted to be represented as the original recipient of the secret lore concerning the heavenly realm, the world to come and the various angels and demons in possession of the Essenes, as, according to Scripture (Gen. v, 24), he was taken alive to heaven after his three hundred and sixty-five years of godly life. Traditions pointing to Babylonian origin singled him out as the possessor of all the hoary wisdom and

---

[1] See Marti, "Comm. to Daniel"; "D. Bibel u. d. Keilschriften," Schrader 3d Ed.; Hilgenfeld, "Die Juedische Apokalyptik"; Kohler, "The Essenes and Apocalyptic Literature" in the *Jewish Quarterly Review* xi, 145 f; Jewish Encyclopedia, art. "Apocalyptic Literature."

knowledge concerning heaven and earth. Besides, ancient folklore clustering around Mount Hermon and the sources of the Jordan picture him as an associate of the angels who interceded in favor of the fallen angels mentioned in Genesis vi, 1-4. Accordingly, numerous visions and fervent appeals to repentance, with incessant cries of woe for the sinners and promises of beatitude for the righteous, were ascribed to him in writings bearing his name. It is a large literature, extending over more than a hundred years, from the time of the Maccabean War to the middle of the first Christian century, but the Hebrew original, and almost the whole Greek translation has been lost, and only an incoherent collection of fragments has been preserved in the Ethiopic language. Being introduced as "the righteous man who saw a vision of the Holy One in heaven and heard from the angels what he was to disclose to remote generations to come, concerning the great Judgment at the end of days," he is first represented as predicting the Flood and admonishing the sinners to repent in time, after he had, as the prophet of God, brought the message of woe and gloom to the fallen angels, declaring that there is no salvation for the wicked and the seducers.

Then speaking in the first person, he describes in Chapters xiv-xix—"the Jewish prototype of Dante"—his journeyings over heaven and earth under the guidance of the archangels. Lifted above the clouds, he beholds the paths of the stars and the lightnings, and the fiery cherubim; then amidst tremors of awe he is admitted into the lofty palace where, in impenetrable flames of fire, the majesty of God is seen on His throne of Glory with the myriads of angels around Him. Beneath a high mountain the place of the whirlwind and of the luminaries comes to sight, and then the ocean and the river of fire, the rivers of Sheol ($=$ Ps. xviii, 5), and the dark abysmal depth whence all the waters of the earth issue forth. There he sees also the corner stone of the earth and the pillars of heaven, and seven mountains of precious stones, of which the middle one eclipses all in brilliancy (Ezek. xxviii, 14). After this he is shown the place of horror in which the seven rebellious star spirits are imprisoned for a thousand years, until the Judgment Day. Farther on he beheld, beneath high mountain rocks, four hollow places, and was told that these were the four apartments of the nether world. Two of these are the temporary abodes of the righteous, one for saintly martyrs like Abel, the other for the simple righteous; they have a spring of water and light. The other two are for the two classes of sinners. The wicked who remained unpunished in life and had an ordinary burial are to remain in this dark realm of pain until the time of the Resurrection, when they will be cast into Gehenna; the others, who suffered a violent death and are now complaining, being neither righteous nor complete sinners, remain in this intermediate state. On hearing this, Enoch cried out, "Blessed be the Lord of righteousness forever!" Turning to the center of the earth, he saw (Chapters xxvi, 1 ff.) the blessed land filled with trees (Palestine), where out of the dismembered tree (exiled Israel) branches had taken new root; and there was Mount Zion with the brook of Siloah beneath, and another mountain with the deep ravine between the two. There he beheld the accursed valley, the gathering place of the ungodly who blasphemed God. Gehinnom, the former place of Moloch sacrifices (Jer. vii, 31), is here designated for the first time in literature as the place of punishment for the wicked, while Sheol is not yet identified with it, as was done afterward in the rabbinical and New Testament writings.

Other visions contained in cosmological and astronomical portions we omit, as being of less concern to us, nor need we dwell on those which present the world's history after certain epochs leading up to the Judgment Day, the advent of the Messiah, and the Resurrection, however interesting for the historian the so-called Beast vision is, in which the seventy nations of the world are pictured as world beasts, and Israel as the flock of God, "the Lord of the Sheep," who first rescues it through Judas Maccabee and finally through the Messiah, "the white bull," to whom all nations will pay homage (Chapters lxxxv-xc). Of greater interest to us is the apocalyptic portion of Chapters xxxvii to lxxi. There the Messiah is announced in Chapters xlv-xlviii, in terms taken from Daniel vii, as the Son of Man coming in the clouds, but not as denoting Israel symbolically, but the words are taken literally to mean that he, God's elect, will come forth from his concealment where he has been kept ever since the world's beginning, "the staff of the righteous and a light to the nations," to be placed by the Ancient of Days, the Lord of the Spirits, upon His throne to judge all the living, angels, men, and nations. He shall consign the wicked, especially the God-defying kings of Israel, such as was the murderous tyrant, king Jannaeus, to eternal punishment in Gehenna, and accord eternal life to the righteous, for whom inexhaustible fountains of wisdom will be opened, to make them shine as the angels in heaven. The names of these, Enoch saw written in the books of life; those of the evildoers, in the books of death. Otherwise he repeatedly claims to have read all the great secrets of the hereafter in the heavenly tablets, showing every event to be predetermined, as was the belief of the Essenes, and he committed them all to his son Methusalah.

Intermingled with Enoch's books are fragments of a *Noah Apocalypse*, in which, in connection with the prediction of the Flood, is also announced the day of visitation of sinners and of a covenant banquet for the righteous, for the latter of which the flesh of the two great monsters, Behemoth and Leviathan (Job xl-xli) will furnish the food, like the primeval ox of the Parsees (Chapters xx, 6-8; 24 comp. iv Ezra. vi, 49; Apoc. Baruch xxix, 4).[2]

The last of the series of Enoch writings is the *"Book of the Secrets of Enoch,"* written originally in Greek, possibly after a Hebrew model, about the middle of the first pre-Christian century, and preserved only in the Slavonic language. Here, too, Enoch tells how he was taken up in his sleep by two angels to the first heaven, where he saw a great sea larger than the earthly sea, and then "the Elders," the two hundred rulers of the stars,

---

[2] "The Book of Enoch," R. H. Charles; Kautsch, "D. Apocryphen u. Pseudepigraphen d. Alt. Test"; Beers' transl. of Enoch; also the books mentioned above in Note 1, and Jewish Encyclopedia s. v. "Enoch."

the treasuries of the snow, the ice, the hoarfrost and the dew under the guardianship of angels, thence to the second heaven, where the fallen angels were imprisoned for whom he had pleaded in vain; and then to the third heaven, where he beheld the celestial Paradise with its tree of life from whose root four streams flowing with honey, milk, wine, and oil issue forth, and its olive tree ever distilling wondrous oil. This, he is told, is the place prepared for the righteous as eternal inheritance. Toward the North he saw the place of torture with its fiery river, its ice and cold, to burn and freeze, and also its pitiless angels, to scourge the various classes of sinners. The sins specified offer a mirror of the vices prevalent then: sodomy, witchcraft, and magic; stealing, lying, slander, envy, lustful thoughts, fornication, and murder; kidnapping, oppression of the poor and cheating them of their possessions; instead of feeding the hungry, allowing them to starve, and instead of clothing them, stripping them naked, and finally the worship of idols, instead of recognizing God as the Creator.

Taken up to the fourth heaven, he saw the sun, the moon, and the four great stars, each moving in their chariots, the sun with its myriads of angels before it, and wondrous phœnixes and flying serpents, seraphlike, accompanying it with songs on its drive Westward to the six great gates, and again, on its coming out of the six gates of the East. The moon also, in its movements through the twelve lunar months of the year, and its equation with the solar months in nineteen years, is described. Of course, we observe here the influence of Greek astronomy.

In the fifth heaven he found the Watchers, the former companions of the fallen angels, in sore distress over the fate of their brethren, but he succeeded in having them resume their song in worship of God. In the sixth heaven he saw the seven orders of angels, foremost the archangels who are appointed over the rest of the angels who direct the movements of the stars and the seasons, the rivers and the seas, fruits and herbs, and finally, those set over the souls of men, taking account of their doings and their lives. They all sing with one voice, accompanied by seven phœnixes, seven cherubim, and seven seraphim, rejoicing before the Lord. Finally, taken up to the seventh heaven, he beheld amidst the radiance of a great light ten classes of angels worshiping the Lord seated on His lofty throne, and singing their "Thrice Holy." But, while his angelic guides dared go no further, nor any of the angels, the archangel Michael took, at God's bidding, his earthly robe from him, and anointed him, and clothed him with the raiment of the Divine Glory, so that he became like one of the glorious angels himself. For thirty days and thirty nights he was here instructed by one of the highest angels in all the secrets of heaven and earth, and he wrote them down in three hundred and sixty-six (three hundred and sixty-five?) days. Nay, more. God himself initiated him, as He had not done to any one even among the angels, into the mysteries of His creation from the beginnings of the universe to those of man, and also regarding the end of the days, so as to comprise the seven millennia of the world. The eight thousand years in Chapter xxiii, 2 seems to be due to Christian interpolation.[3] He also told him that these books of mysteries shall remain under angelic guardianship until the time has come for their disclosure.[4] Being a Hellenistic product, the Slavonic Enoch omits the Messiah and the Resurrection, and instead accentuates the immortality, and also the preëxistence, of the soul (xxxiii, 5).

In place of the antediluvian Enoch, the Alexandrian Essenes, more versed in Greek literature, took the Sibyl, the ancient heathen prophetess, known for her gloomy foretellings to many lands, as a type of an apocalyptic seer and preacher. Interspersing numerous oracles which circulated under the name of the Chaldean and Etrurian Sibyl in their writings, they represented her as Noah's daughter-in-law announcing the imminent Flood and at the same time warning the people to repent, as did also Noah, according to the Talmudic tradition (Sanhedrin 90[a] f), in order that they escape their impending doom. In the main, however, this was, as in the case of Enoch, merely the prelude to the appeal to all coming generations, that is, the heathen nations, to repent of their sins, particularly of the three capital sins, idolatry, murder, specifically infanticide, adultery or sodomy, and to become true worshipers of the Only One and holy God, lest perdition would overtake them. With great emphasis, she dwells on the great Judgment Day which would consign the wicked to the fire of hell (the

---

[3] The seven heavens recur also in the vision of Levi in the Testaments of the Twelve Patriarchs (Levi ii, 3), and the cosmology is nearly the same. So also in the Talmud Hagigah 12[b] f.

[4] See "The Book of the Secrets of Enoch," Morfill and Charles (1896).

Tartarus), to the fire of the world conflagration which would consume the entire present world, to make way for the new, which is to offer salvation and bliss to the righteous under the reign of God's anointed King (= the Messiah).

These Sibylline Books, however, were lost sight of by the Jews and left in the hands of Christian writers, who not only appropriated them and gave them, by interpolations and alterations, a Christian character, but also added new books to the original Jewish ones, and disarranged their order, so as to make the reconstruction of the whole literature most difficult to the student. Strange to say, the Sibyl became a prominent figure in Church history down to the Middle Ages, but was altogether forgotten by the Jews. It is sufficient for our purpose to summarize a few of the books.

The oldest one, belonging to the Maccabean time, consisted originally of Book i, 1-323 and Book iii, 97-828. It presents, like one of the visions of Enoch, the history of the world from creation to the end of times in ten periods, the last of which was to be ushered in by the fall of Rome, as the fourth world kingdom doomed, as is Syria in Daniel's vision, to perdition at the advent of the Messiah. The biblical story of Genesis down to the building of the Tower of Babel is here strangely combined with Greek mythology, particularly with Hesiod's theogony, and so are the builders of the Babel Tower identified with the Greek Titans, and the three sons of Noah paralleled with Saturn, Titan, and Japetus. Adam's name is oddly connected with Hades, as the death of the first man implied his entrance there, whereas

Paradise is to be the future land of immortality. We furthermore come across a number of Greek concepts, such as the river Acheron and the Acherusian Lake, which influenced the medieval visions of the Inferno down to Dante. It pictures the Messianic future in glowing colors, and its prophetic tone probably inspired Vergil in his portraiture of the Augustan age in his Eclogues iv.

The other Sibylline Books identify the Elysian Fields with Paradise, and tell of the three rivers of wine, milk, and honey flowing there, also mentioned in the Slavonic Enoch book, as well as of the biblical Manna awaiting the righteous. The Essenic origin of these books, despite the current opinion to the contrary, cannot be doubted, as such passages as iii 591 f and iv, 26, 64, referring to the rites of bathing in living waters for worship and for conversion, and also those in iii, 235 ff. and ii, 322 ff., extolling the virtue of justice, poverty, and disinterested, helpful love, amply show. Worth mentioning is at least the strange episode concerning the anti-Christ in the person of Nero, who was expected to reappear as the very embodiment of hostile Rome, to come back from the far-off East, the alter-Ego of Satan or Belial, to antagonize the Messiah, but only to meet final defeat at his hand (Book iv, 119-138; v, 28 f., 155 f., 215 f., 363 f.; viii, 151 f., 337 f.; xii, 78 f.). The fourth book is a strong appeal to the heathen world to forsake idolatry and by a renewal of their whole being by bathing in living streams, to enter the fold of Judaism.

More important for us here is the remarkable passage

in ii, 253-313, in which the various classes of sinners and their punishments are far more elaborately described than in the Slavonic Enoch, x, 4-6. They became henceforth the standing theme in the Christian Apocalypses down to Dante's Inferno. The writer had probably the Orphic visions as models before him, but the Jewish character is evident. The passage reads in full: "All have to pass the fiery stream, the unquenchable flame. The righteous will all be saved, but the wicked will perish forever, whosoever have perpetrated evil before: The murderers and their abettors, the liars and thieves, the fraudulent and the spendthrifts, the adulterers and the tricksters, the backbiters, and the arrogant, the lawless, the idolators, and those who apostatized from the great, undying God, the blasphemers, and the oppressors of the pious; the enemies of the faith and the slayers of the saints; the deceitful and double-faced, the elders who seem venerable before men's eyes, but act unjustly from fear of men, allowing themselves to be guided by false rumors, more dangerous than panthers and wolves, the worst of men, however greatly they elate themselves above others! Likewise the usurers who accumulate interest upon interest in their houses, and those who afflict orphans and widows, whether sharing their ill-gotten gain with them or vexing them when giving them of their own; those also who forsake their parents in old age, failing to compensate them for what they received from them, even for their education, and showing disobedience and contradicting them in unseeming words; they also who deny the goods they received in trust; the servants who rose against their masters; they who have polluted their own body in lustful sin as well as those who violated pure virgins or commingled with women in secret; those who committed abortion and they who exposed their infants to death, and the poisoners among men or women. All these will the wrath of the heavenly God lead to the stream of fire, and His angels will scourge them with fiery chains, and cast them before the fierce monsters of hell, and fiery wheels will turn them round about. Lamenting over their terrible lot, the fathers over their young children, the mothers over their sucklings, they will fill these ghastly spaces with howling cries. Suffering thrice for their evildoings, they shall be consumed by fearful thirst and bitter woe, gnashing their teeth and longing for death which will never come, and it will be too late for repentance which is given only for the seven decades (ages) of life." Obviously we have here a portraiture of the vices and crimes prevalent at the time, and the writer pours out his wrath of indignation against his contemporaries, especially against the hypocrites, sparing his own kinsmen as little as did Dante in his Inferno.

It is easy to see how the Roman oppression and particularly the Romanizers on the Jewish throne, King Herod and his sons, brought about a reaction in Judea which opposed the apotheosis of Enoch—though in the later Cabala Henoch-Metatron became God's charioteer, like the Persian Mithra. So Abraham, the Jewish ancestor, became the typical seer and possessor of all wisdom in Enoch's place. Accordingly, *the Apocalypse of Abraham* describes his ascent to heaven with reference to Genesis, Chapter xv, where the words, "He brought him forth outside" (Verse 5) were interpreted: "He lifted him above the firmament to look down upon the stars and the world beneath." Speaking in the first person, the patriarch relates first all about his conversion from idolatry to pure monotheism, and then how, after having offered the fourfold sacrifice, which was to symbolize the downfall of the four world kingdoms preparatory to the Messianic era, he was carried by the highest of the angels, named Yahoel, upon the wing of the untouched bird to the uppermost heaven. There he beheld amidst a radiant light the four holy creatures of Ezekiel carrying the throne chariot of God. Looking down from here, he saw the seventh heaven with its multitude of angels, its light, and its dew (of resurrection), and then the sixth and the fifth heaven, where all the stars are located. And there lay beneath him the earth with its inhabitants, the men with their righteous and ungodly deeds, and the sea with its great monsters, and then hell with its torments for the wicked, and the Garden of Eden with its blessed trees and its food for the righteous. Mankind was divided into two opposite parts, the people of God on the *right* and the idolaters on the *left;* the former to be saved after the great judgment, the latter to enter the realm of doom together with the archfiend, Azazel. In the Garden of Eden he beheld Adam and Eve, and, besides them, Cain in league with the Adversary, round about whom were the different vices such as impurity, jealousy, evil desire, and idolatry with its Moloch sacrifices, while pure worship of God and Prayer were on the other side.

After this the patriarch was shown the destruction of the Temple by the Romans, and he received the information that the age of ungodliness would last twelve hours—that is twelve hundred years, from David to Titus—and the age of righteousness would be ushered in only after the divine judgment upon the heathen nations shall have been executed through his (Abraham's) seed. Ten plagues, as at Israel's deliverance from Egypt, shall be visited upon the godless world, forming the so-called birthpangs of the Messiah, and then blasts of the heavenly trumpet will herald forth the advent of God's elect, who, endowed with divine powers, will summon the scattered and despised people of God to the Holy City for their eternal possession, the number of the righteous to be saved having been predetermined in heaven. Their oppressors and foes shall be consumed in the fire of Hades.

This apocalyptic book, discovered only in recent times in its Slavonic garb, was originally written in Hebrew and translated into Greek, and its contents are reflected in the rabbinical literature as well as in the Baruch Apocalypse, iv, 4, and iv Ezra, iii, 14.

We omit discussing these two Apocalypses, written amidst the uttermost woe and despair of the people after the destruction of the Temple, with the view of offering them solace and hope by the announcement that this world is fast approaching its end and that the world of resurrection and eternal life is at hand. The large eschatological material contained therein is rather beyond our scope. Neither shall we expatiate on the somewhat older apocalyptic book entitled *"Assumptio*

Moses" (= "the Taking up of Moses"), in which Moses as "the mediator between God and Israel" announces "the Day of Visitation" for the latter end of the fifth millennium, which would place the Messianic era in the sixth millennium. The main portion of the book, which must have contained the visionary journey of Moses along the heavens, and which is alluded to in the Midrash (Sifre Deuteronomy xxxiv, 1 f.) and in the Baruch Apocalypse lxxvi, has evidently been lost.

So we close this chapter with the highly instructive Testament of Abraham,[5] an Alexandrian product of the first Christian century. In poetic form, the aged patriarch, the friend of God and benefactor of men, is portrayed here as rebelling at first against the fate of mortality and submitting to it only after having received the promise of being permitted to survey the entire universe before his death. Thus, he is taken by the archangel, Michael, in his heavenly chariot to the heights of the firmament, where he looks down upon the earth with its inhabitants. But then, as he observes the doings of people, the murder, the adultery, and the burglary they commit, he is horrified, and in his rage he asks the archangel to smite the malefactors with instant death, and the archangel is bound to obey. But there a voice of heaven is heard saying: "O archangel, Michael, stop thy chariot and turn Abraham away, lest, seeing all living in wickedness, he destroy all creation. For, sinless as he is, he has no pity for sinners, whereas I who am the Maker of the world do not wish to destroy a single creature of Mine, but defer death until he repent

[5] Jewish Encyclopedia, art. "Abraham, Testament of."

and live. Go, therefore, and show Abraham the judgments and the retribution behind the Eastern (Western?) gate of heaven that he may have compassion on the souls of the sinners whom he killed in his wrath." With these words of incomparable beauty and grandeur, the like of which have never been spoken by any prophet since the days of Ezekiel, God sends Abraham with the archangel to view Hell and Paradise. A grand scene opens here before the gaze of the patriarch. Two roads, one wide and one narrow, stretch on either side, ending at two gates correspondingly large and small. A large procession of souls is led by angels along the former, and a few walk along the other. In front of the two gates Adam, of majestic appearance, sits on a golden throne watching, now weeping and tearing his hair in distress at the sight of the multitude going through the wide gate, and then smiling and exulting at the sight of the few entering the narrow gate. For, while the one leads to destruction and the other to eternal bliss, against seven thousands walking on the road of doom there is hardly one soul walking on the path of righteousness without blemish. Following the proceeding of the judgment of the souls, Abraham sees the scourging angels driving thousands through the wide gate to perdition with their tongs of fire, while he beholds a single soul being led by one angel to the middle space. Farther on he sees Abel, the martyr son of Adam, seated on a throne of crystal, and before him a crystal table with an immense scroll in which the actions of men are recorded by two angels holding pen and ink in their hands.—In another version of the book,

Enoch is named as the heavenly recorder, like Thoth, the Egyptian scribe of the gods.—On the other side one angel holds a pair of scales to weigh actions, and another fierce-looking angel holds a vessel of fire to probe the souls. Much puzzled as Abraham is by the sight of Abel in this high position, he is told: " 'Man shall be judged by man,' says the law (Gen. ix, 6); only at the final judgment, which is everlasting and unchangeable, God himself shall preside, and the twelve tribes of Israel will be judged first (Comp. Yalkut to Dan. § 1064), and then all creation will be judged by the Ruler of all at the end of time."

The culmination of this wondrous vision is reached by the following striking episode. One single soul is being brought before Abel, and as the scroll is opened, there, behold, the number and weight of the evil and the good deeds of the soul are found to be exactly alike. So the soul is neither handed over to chastisement, nor to salvation, but placed in the middle state. Then Abraham, on learning that the soul was to remain there until God at the end of time decides its fate, says to the archangel: "Let us offer a prayer on its behalf," and as both pray, there appears a light-encircled angel who brings the soul to Paradise amidst the praise and thanksgiving of the patriarch. After having thus been made aware of the power of prayerful intercession on behalf of this one soul, Abraham proceeds, amidst pangs of remorse and tears, to invoke God's forgiveness for all the souls of the sinners whom he had so rashly consigned to perdition, and God grants his request and restores the dead to life. It is unnecessary to give here the rest of the story of the Apocalypse. Suffice it to say that, after further arguments and information concerning death, Abraham's soul is carried by the angels into Paradise, where the various saints have their mansions of bliss assigned to them.

It must be noted here that there is nowhere in the book any trace of the belief in Adam's fall and the original sin, nor any allusion to Christ and his atoning power. In other words, the assumption of the Christian character of the Apocalypse is contradicted by its contents. On the contrary, the passage in Matthew vii, 13-14, speaking of the wide and narrow gate has its source right here. Evidently Egyptian and Persian ideas have influenced the author, but he invested them with the spirit of the ancient prophets and created a work which deserves to be read by all who wish to obtain the right knowledge of Judaism in its eschatological aspect.[7]

[7] James, "Testament of Abraham"; Kohler, "The Pre-Talmudic Haggada" in the *Jewish Quarterly Review*, vii, 581-606; Jewish Encyclopedia, art. "Abraham, Testament of."

CHAPTER VI

GEHENNA AND PARADISE IN THE APOCALYPTIC LITERA-
TURE OF THE NEW TESTAMENT

This is not the place for a critical estimate of the New Testament as a historical source, and still less of the personality of Jesus, concerning whom the opinions of scholars differ as widely as do the conflicting records in the gospels. Still, we cannot avoid considering several important questions in dealing with the great subject. There is, first of all, the authorship of the gospels and their sources, which demand consideration, since neither Jesus nor any of his apostles, except Paul, who never saw him alive, wrote a word of what we have in the New Testament. Like his disciples, Jesus spoke Aramaic, whereas the New Testament presents his sayings and all the traditions about him in the Greek language. Only three words of his have been preserved in the Aramaic, two in Mark v, 41 and vii, 34, spoken by him at the healing of a sick child and of a deaf and dumb person, and probably regarded by the writer as a magic formula, and a third one in Mark xv, 35 and Matthew xxvii, 46, the famous outburst of despair at the agony of death on the cross: *"Eli, Eli, lama shabachtani"* (= "My God, my God, why hast Thou forsaken me"), the Aramaic translation of Psalm xxii, 2, which ill accords with the foretelling of his tragic end and ascribed to him in numerous passages throughout the gospels. Quite significantly Luke xxiii, 46 (comp. Acts vii, 59), has instead the Psalm (xxxi, 6): "Father, in Thy hand I commend my spirit," while the late Gospel of Peter translates the former one: "My power, my power, thou hast forsaken me," as if the divine Christ thus addressed his human, or fleshly, self, he himself having suffered no pain, as the heretic sect called Docetæ, "the Semblancer," assumed. It stands to reason that during the two generations when the original sayings of, and the traditions about, Jesus were translated into Greek, many legends sprang up to color and obscure the historical character of his personality whose very greatness consisted in his simple and tender humanity.

But there is another point which concerns us here most. It is to-day generally recognized by the scholarly world that the religious movement which was started by John the Baptist's call to the people to wash themselves clean of their sins in the waters of the Jordan and repent in preparation for the kingdom of God that was nigh,[1] and which culminated in the proclamation of Jesus as the Messiah by his Galilean followers at Jerusalem, originated and centered in the Jewish eschatology as developed and shaped by the Apocalyptists since Daniel and Enoch. Only in these circles the end of this world and the beginning of a new one were looked for, with a view to the advent of the Messiah as the "Son of Man" and the judge of the souls after

---

[1] See Jewish Encyclopedia, art. "John the Baptist."

or before the Resurrection. And here the question necessarily occurs to thinking readers, whether the simple fishermen and herdsmen of Galilee, among whom Peter and John, the most prominent disciples of Jesus, are characterized in Acts iv, 13, as "unlearned and ignorant men," could ever have understood those eschatological terms such as is the Messianic "Son of Man" of Enoch used by Jesus in addressing them? True to his declaration, "I was not sent but unto the lost sheep of the house of Israel" (Matt. xv, 24 comp. xviii, 12 and Luke xv, 4 f,), he made it his life task to bring home the good tidings of salvation by righteousness to the outcast and despised, neglected by the Pharisean schoolmen, while they in turn lifted him in their grateful homage at first to the station of a prophet, and at last to that of a Messiah. None of the dozen and more passages representing him as having spoken of himself as the Son of Man in the sense of the Messiah, is, accordingly, to be taken as genuine. They merely betray the hand of such Essenic writers as had joined the early Christian movement, eager to identify Jesus with their Messianic concepts.[2]

Especially illuminating, therefore, are the twenty-fourth and twenty-fifth chapters of Matthew. Leaving aside the introduction in Matthew xxiv, 1-5, and parallels in Mark and Luke and a few slight alterations or additions, the original Jewish character of the Apocalypse—in which even the Sabbath rest is accentuated in v. 20—is self-evident. It plainly refers, not to the apostles, but to the Jewish nation preparing the same

[2] Jewish Encyclopedia, art. "Jesus."

for the great crisis, the so-called "birth-throes" or "travail" of the Messianic time in which Daniel's "Abomination of Desolation," the symbol of heathenism, and the attack of the heathen nations upon Jerusalem, as well as the false Messiahs, were to play a conspicuous rôle before the final triumph to be brought about by the Son of Man. Likewise is the parable of the wise and foolish virgins, and that of the faithful and slothful servants (xxv, 1-20, comp. Luke xii, 35-40, where the Son of Man is especially mentioned) of Jewish, or, more particularly, of Essenic origin, as can be learned from the almost identical and contemporary one in the Talmud (Shabbath 153ᵃ). Even the idea of a marriage or covenant feast in the hereafter is originally Jewish, referring to the reunion of God and Israel as based on Isaiah xlv, 1 and xlviii, 12 (comp. Pesik R. xli; Aboth iii, 16 and Rev. xix, 9).

Still more significant is the second Apocalypse xxv, 31-46, in which the Messiah as the Son of Man and the judge of the nations is portrayed as sitting as King on God's throne of glory with all the angels around him. Placing the sheep—that is, as in Enoch, the righteous ones—on his right hand, and the goats, the unrighteous, on the left, he shall say to those on his right: "Come, ye blessed of my father, inherit the kingdom prepared for you from the foundation of the world. For I was hungered and ye gave me meat; I was thirsty, and ye gave me drink. I was a stranger, and ye took me in; naked, and ye clothed me; I was in prison, and ye came unto me" (probably to be corrected into "ye ransomed me"). And then in answer to their questioning he shall say: "Verily inasmuch as ye did it unto one of these my brethren, even the least, ye did it unto me." Turning then to those on the left, he shall say: "Depart from me, ye cursed, into the eternal fire which is prepared for the devil and his angels!" while reproaching them for having failed to practice charity in the way the righteous did.   Now this whole address of Jesus to his brethren in the name of his Father is but a substitute for the original Judgment of God and His Anointed, Enoch's "Son of Man."   Moreover, the Midrash to Psalm cxviii, 17, has preserved for us the reference to the biblical source on which the whole Apocalypse was based: "Open unto me the gates of righteousness that I may enter."   This refers to the world to come, when man, on being asked for his meritorious acts, will say: "I gave the hungry to eat, I gave the thirsty to drink, I clothed the naked, brought up the fatherless, aided the poor, and practiced this or that charity," and he will be admitted among the righteous.   Likewise, does God, according to the Midrash (Aggadath Shir ha Shirim to Song of Songs IV, 1), say to Israel: "In practicing charity you do it unto Me, for I am in no need of bread, but as you give it to the poor, you give it unto Me."

Of particular importance, however, is the Apocalypse contained in the *"Book of Revelation"* of John the Divine, the last book of the New Testament,[3] which, while being connected and interwoven with the Letters addressed to the Seven Churches of Asia by John the Presbyter on the isle of Patmos, underwent such radical changes that its original Jewish character has not been

---

[3] See Jewish Encyclopedia, art. "Revelation, Book of."

recognized by the commentators, with the exception of Vischer and Harnack, notwithstanding its utter incongruity with the New Testament concept of Jesus and its decided nationalism and Hebraism. Beginning with Chapter iv, 1, and ending with xxii, 7, it has obviously been written by one of the Essenic zealots during the last days of the siege of Jerusalem by the Romans, betraying the very same Messianic views voiced soon afterward by the authors of the Baruch and Ezra Apocalypses. The seer starts with a theophany similar to that of Isaiah vi, Ezekiel, and Daniel, only adding to Ezekiel's four living creatures twenty-four Elders—probably taken from some Babylonian source—the heavenly court surrounding God's throne of glory. There he sees in God's right hand a scroll with seven seals to be opened only by the Lion of Judah, the root of David. The opening of the first four seals by the Jewish Messiah—for whom the Christian editor substituted the Slain Lamb—announces the four horsemen: War, symbolized by the victorious Parthian bowman, Strife, Famine, and Pestilence, and the fifth, Persecutions. At the sight of these the seer beholds the souls of the Jewish martyrs under God's altar (Comp. Aboth d. R. N. xxvi) and hears their cry: "How long, O Ruler, dost Thou leave our blood unavenged?" but they are told to have patience yet, for more numerous will be the victims. The opening of the sixth seal announces earthquakes, eclipses of sun and moon, falling stars, and other disturbances of heaven—exactly as in the abovementioned Apocalypse of Matthew and parallels—and finally the seventh announces, as specially heralded by seven trumpets, numerous plagues similar to the Egyptian ones, then a star sending forth poisonous Wormwood, so as to smite the third part of the land, the sea and rivers, and also sun, moon and stars.   These were to be followed by three great woes, the one coming in the shape of ferocious beasts, more so than in those of Joel ii and iii, sent forth from the very depth of the abyss, called *Abaddon*, to torment the inhabitants of the earth.   In protection against the plague twelve thousand saints of each of the twelve tribes of Israel were to have their foreheads marked by the seal of God, and they were afterward to form the nucleus of the Messianic Kingdom at the Millennium.   The second woe was to come from the river Euphrates, whence the invincible Parthian armies would invade the land and slay a third part of mankind, but the rest would by no means repent of their sins of idolatry, murder, fornication, and theft.   Finally "the great secret of God," the world's end, with its good tidings for God's faithful servants, will reach its fulfillment.   As in Daniel's vision, the seer now beholds the siege of the Holy City and its Temple lasting three and a half years.   During this time two prophets, like Elijah and Moses, displaying miraculous powers, would preach repentance in sackcloth, but in the end succumb to the heathen foe, then to be taken up to heaven amidst a mighty earthquake in which seven thousand men would perish, and finally the Holy City would fall into the hands of the heathen.

The great judgment to come upon Rome, however, is preceded by two grand scenes in heaven (Ch. xii to xiii) borrowed from a Babylonian myth.   The seer beholds first Zion, the mother of the Messiah, pursued by Satan, the primeval dragon, and forced to flee before giving birth to her son, "who is to rule all the nations with a rod of iron" (= the Messiah of Psalm ii, 9), and who will remain in concealment until the time arrives for his appearance on earth. Then again Satan is seen in battle array against Michael, the guardian angel of Israel, who finally hurls him down to the earth, thereby deciding the fate of Satanic Rome. To this must be referred the saying of Jesus in Luke x, 18: "I beheld Satan falling as lightning from heaven."

Rome herself is now seen coming forth out of the sea in the shape of a beast with seven heads and ten horns, as depicted in Daniel vii, 4 f., uttering blasphemies against God and His temple and making war against His saints, while all dwellers on earth worship it. And this is followed by another beast coming up out of the earth, exercising the authority of the first beast, deceiving all men by having them bear the mark or the name of that first beast on their right hand and forehead, while at the same time it displays miraculous powers. Of course, the first beast is Rome situated on seven hills, having had seven kings from Augustus to Titus, but identified with the demonic emperor, Nero Redivivus, the incarnation of Belial or Satan, the name given in Hebrew ciphers as 666 (= corresponding to Neron Cæsar); the other beast represents the imperial priesthood which deified the emperors of Rome whose very image on the coins was regarded as a matter of horror and abomination by the rigorous Essenes.

While the doom of both Rome and the worshipers

of the emperors is announced in heaven, there the Son
of Man in the clouds comes to sight, having a golden
crown on his head and a sharp sickle in his hand, with
which he is to gather the vintage of the earth for the
great wine press of the wrath of God (comp. Joel iv, 13)
and, in place of God in Isaiah lxiii, 2-6, he is arrayed in
a garment sprinkled with blood (Ch. xiv, 14; xix, 11).
Seven bowls of the divine wrath are then poured out
upon the worshipers of the beast and its throne, upon
the sea and rivers and the sun above, and also upon the
Parthian armies allied with the mythical Nero coming
from the East.   But the last bowl of the divine wrath
brings about the final judgment, signaled by an earthquake "such as was not since there were men on earth."
As over Babylon of old in Isaiah xxi, 9, the voice resounding through the heavens is heard crying forth:
"Fallen, fallen is Babylon the great, and is to become
the habitation of demons."   Rome, drunken with the
blood of the saintly martyrs, "the harlot that sitteth upon
many waters" who had made the kings of the earth
drunken with the wine of her fornication, is now to drain
the cup of the wine of the fierceness of God's wrath.
The merchant princes of the world shall wail over the
fall of the great city whose ships were upon all the seas,
laden with the treasures of the earth (xvii-xix).   But
above it the heavenly powers will shout forth their Hallelujah!   Salvation and glory to God who in His judgment has avenged the blood of His servants!   And the
birds that fly in midheaven shall be bidden to gather together for the great feast of God to eat the flesh of the
kings and the mighty men and their horses and the men.

The beast and the false prophet and their armies that made war against the Messiah and his army will be cast into the lake of fire, while the victors in heaven and on earth sing a new song of triumph besides the song of Moses (xv and xix).

Then Satan will also be cast down into the abyss and be chained there (like Azazel in the book of Enoch) for a thousand years (xx). This is the Messianic millennium, for which the Ezra Apocalypse (vii, 28) has four hundred years, whereas the Talmud Sanhedrin, 99a, offers reasons for figuring both four hundred and one thousand years. During this time the one hundred and forty-four thousand saints who formed the kernel of the army of the Messiah will reign as priests with him. In place of the ruined city a new Jerusalem will be rebuilt of sapphires, rubies, and emeralds, as pictured in Isaiah liv, 11 f., and Tobit xii, 6; xiv, 5, with its streets of pure gold, its twelve gates of pearl, in accordance with the twelve tribes of Israel, and its foundations of precious stones like those twelve precious stones of the high priest's breast shield of yore (xxi). The ark of old will again be brought to sight (xi, 19). God will have His Shekinah there, and His glory will be there for a light. His servants will see Him face to face like Moses of yore, and the heathen nations that will have escaped the universal doom will walk in His light, and bring their wealth into it.

But, after the end of the millennium, Satan will be released again out of his prison—exactly as was the Parsee belief—and he will induce the armies of Gog and Magog (of Ezekiel xxxviii-xxxix), numberless as the sands of the sea, to encamp around the Holy City and wage the final war against Israel. The battle is to take place in Har Magedon (xvii, 16), (probably the Hamon-Gog of Ezekiel xxxix, 11-17), but they will be consumed by the fire of heaven (Ezek. 5, 6 ff.). Then Satan, the great deceiver, will be cast into the lake of fire to be tormented there forever. With him Hades and Death will be cast down, and the earth and the sea will give up their dead; for the last Judgment is to be held by God himself after the general resurrection. In place of the first heaven and the first earth and sea, a new heaven and a new earth will then arise (= Is. lxv, 17; lxvi, 22), and a new Jerusalem will come down from heaven like a bride adorned for God as His spouse (Is. lxi, 5). A river of the water of life proceeding from the throne of God will be in the midst of the streets to feed the tree of life, which will have twelve kinds of fruit for the twelve months of the year, and whose leaves will be for the healing of the nations (Ezk. lxvii, 12). No unclean one, nor any sinner will enter the city, whose name shall be "The Lord is there" (Ezek. lxviii, 35).

Such are in the main the contents of this remarkable Apocalypse, obviously written at the very height of the great tragedy of the Jewish nation. It evidences, as Mommsen in his History of Rome (v 521 f., Germ. Ed.) has well stated, the author's intense hatred of Rome, and likewise the abhorrence of the deification of her emperors, whose images were as loathsome to the zealot, as was the idol of Antiochus Epiphanes to the Maccabean saints. Never could the Neronic persecutions of the Christians in Rome have provoked such vehement ire and fury against heathenism as is voiced here at the very time when the Church endeavored to win over the heathen world. But aside from this, the outlook of the Apocalypse upon a future which is centered upon Jerusalem as the capital of the twelve tribes of Israel, while the worshipers of God from among the heathens play only a secondary rôle, strongly contrasts with the view expressed in those passages which speak of a world conquest by Christianity under the Messiahship of the slain Lamb (after Is. lxi, 7; comp. Acts viii, 32.) The Christian editor not only substituted the Lamb for the Lion of Judah, and the Christian saints and martyrs for those of the Jewish people, but went so far as to accord to Jesus titles such as "the first and the last," "the alpha and omega," and the praises befitting God alone. He also made so many alterations and interpolations in the original as to disarrange the entire order and dislocate numerous passages. This editor, probably John the Presbyter himself, a declared antagonist of Paulinian Christianity which he places on a level with the idolatrous practices of Balaam and Jezebel (Ch. ii, 5; 14; 20), apparently felt called upon to adapt the Jewish Apocalypse—which, written in Hebrew or Aramaic, seemingly had a large circulation among the Essenes and Judeo-Christians—to the views and doctrines of the Church, notwithstanding its nationalistic character. Henceforth the "Book of Revelation" became the common property of the Church. By Dante, however, as by the medieval writers in general, the book was ascribed to John the Apostle, to whom, as the type of divine love, the highest place in heaven is assigned in the Paradiso xxv, 94, where the very words of the Apocalypse vii, 9, are quoted. But the whole aspect of the heavenly Jerusalem is based upon this Apocalypse.

Before discussing the Apocalypses of Peter and Paul, which exerted a determining influence on the Inferno and Paradiso of Dante and on his medieval predecessors, it may not be amiss to dwell briefly on the doctrine of Christ's descent to Hades, which formed part of the apostolic symbol or creed, and has found a conspicuous place at the very beginning of the Inferno iv, 50-59. To the believer in the divinity of Jesus, the story of his death and his bodily resurrection on the third day was naturally more or less offensive. Thus, at an early period, the belief arose that his going down to the realm of the departed was not an ordinary death, but was a voluntary act of his, done with a view to release the spirits imprisoned there, to make them partake, by his preaching, of his salvation (I Petri iii, 19; iv, 6). The same idea is expressed in the Ephesians iv, 8-10, where the Psalm (Verse lxviii, 19): Thou hast ascended on high and hast led captivity captive and received gifts among men—applied by R. Akiba to Moses (Shabbath 89ᵃ)—refers to Jesus as having descended unto the lower parts of the earth, and from there ascended above all the heavens "to take the captives and give gifts unto men." Accordingly, the apocryphal Gospel of Peter (v, 10) tells that Jesus, when rising out of the tomb and reaching to the uppermost heaven, is addressed by the heavenly voice: "Hast thou preached to them that sleep?" and his answer is given from the cross: "Yea." A full description of the descent is given in the apocryphal Gospel of Nicodemus ii, 10, according to which Jesus, as the Lord of Glory of Psalm xxiv, 7-10, enters Hades in human shape to seize Satan and hand him over chained to Hades, to keep him secure until his second coming. He, then, delivers Adam and all his descendants, with the help of the cross suspended in Hades, and takes them with him to Paradise, giving them in charge of the archangel, Michael, while they are met by Enoch and Elijah. Likewise has the Christian portion of the apocalyptic Ascensio Isaiac Chapters vi to xi, a "Vision of Isaiah" belonging to the second century, in which the prophet is represented as having ascended up to the seven heavens, where he first beheld Adam, Abel, Seth, Enoch, and the rest of the righteous. Above this he sees a light more radiant than anywhere in the other heavens, encircling the Trinity, the unnamable God of Glory in the center, Jesus, glorious like Him, at His right, and the angel of the spirit (= the Holy Ghost) at His left. There he heard the voice of the Most High telling Jesus to go down, descending through all the heavens beneath, until he reaches the firmament, where the ruler of this world, that is Satan, resides, and then enter unknown the forecourt of Hades, which is the Limbo of the medieval writers, but not Gehenna. There he should remain for three days. The real object of this descent, however, is not stated in the apocalyptic fragment. While the Church Fathers differ as to the souls that were redeemed by the descent of Jesus, Dante follows the generally accepted doctrine that the Old

Testament worthies were released by Jesus from the Limbo and taken up with him to Paradise.

The so-called Apocalypse of Peter, known at the close of the second century as such, was found in the year 1886 in fragmentary form together with a part of the apocryphal Gospel of Peter and a portion of the "Book of Enoch" on a little parchment scroll deposited in a tomb at Achmin in Upper Egypt, and the discovery of those two unknown writings created a great stir throughout the scholarly world. As Albert Dieterich, in his work, "Nekyiah," well suggests, the scroll containing these eschatological portions was, like the ancient Egyptian tomb deposits, placed there as a talisman for the dead. Among the many writers who discussed these "relics of the earliest Christian Apocalypses," Montague Rhodes James of Cambridge, England, says that "the Apocalypse of Peter had a share in the moulding of the greatest poem of the Middle Ages, the 'Divina Commedia,'" taking it to be the source, not merely of the Apocalypse of Paul, but also of the second book of the Sibyllines, which we have shown in the former chapter to be mainly a Jewish work. On closer examination the Apocalypse proves to be, as maintained by Dieterich, a compilation of older material rather than an original unit. It apparently consists of three parts artificially connected. The beginning is taken over, though not literally, from the eschatological address ascribed to Jesus in Matthew xxiv-xxv and parallels discussed before. It must be noted, however, that the words "the sons of perdition" and the "sons of lawlessness," corresponding with the Hebrew of *Sons of Belial*, are used in the Epistles and not in the Synoptic Gospels. The following vision of the two men, "shining with the radiant beauty of angels" and standing before Jesus on the mount, and also of the place of the righteous in heaven, "luminous like the sun and fragrant with the perfume of wondrous plants and spices," shown the apostles by Jesus at their request, appears to be a comment on, or another version of, the story of the transfiguration (Matt. xvii, 2, Mark ix, 2); particularly so of Luke ix, 28. There Moses and Elijah appeared to the three apostles as communing with Jesus. Their aspect was so dazzling that Peter asked whether they should not have a screen or tabernacle to be able to bear the overawing sight. At any rate, the Christian Apocalyptist found in the story an opportunity of describing briefly the place of the *former* righteous men and their glory in Paradise. Far larger is the description of the place of chastisement and of those that were being chastised by the dark appareled angels, seen by the writer directly opposite to the paradise. There is nothing in this whole portion to indicate a Christian origin. First there are those that "blaspheme the way of righteousness," and these are seen hanging by their tongues, while the flaming fire torments them from beneath. Then there are those who pervert righteousness, seen in a great lake of burning mire tormented by angels. A third class are women hung by their hair over the bubbling mire, because they adorned themselves for adultery, whereas the adulterers were hanging by their feet with their heads in the mire. A fourth class consisted of murderers and those who had conspired with them; they were cast into a pit full of evil reptiles by which they were smitten and tormented, while their victims stood by them and, seeing their punishment, cried forth: "O God, righteous is Thy Judgment!"   A fifth class was formed by mothers who destroyed their children and caused abortion; they were seen in a pit filled with the gore and filth that ran down from them and rose up to their throats, while the children who thus died, born before their due time, cried out against them.   A sixth class were those that had persecuted the righteous and delivered them up; they had fire up to the middle of their body, while they were scourged by evil spirits and had their entrails devoured by worms that rested not (= Is. lxvi, 24).   A seventh class who had blasphemed and spoken evil of "the way of righteousness" were seen gnawing their lips and receiving red-hot iron upon their eyes.   An eighth class was made up of false witnesses, who were seen gnawing their tongues and having flaming fire in their mouths.   A ninth class were the wealthy who had no pity upon the orphans and widows, thus neglecting "the commandment of God"; they were seen, clad in filthy rags, rolling upon pebbles sharper than swords and spits.   A tenth class was formed by usurers who stood in a lake of pitch and blood and boiling mire up to their knees.   An eleventh class was hurled down from a great cliff and carried up again to be hurled down anew in ceaseless turns.   These were those who had polluted their bodies, the men by sodomy, the women by a similar perversion of nature.   A twelfth class consisted of worshipers of idols in place of God.   A thirteenth class smote each other incessantly with iron rods. . . .   Here is a làcuna, but it has been well suggested that the missing words stated that these were the quarrelsome and pugnacious ones, bent upon hurting their fellow-men. The fourteenth and last class were seen burning and being roasted, while turning about in the great flame; these were those who had forsaken "the way of God."

We have here, then, the punishments to be the exact retribution of the various sins on the principle of measure for measure as found in all ancient systems of legislation and applied to the hereafter, as we have seen, in the Orphic and Pythagorean eschatology, in Plato and Vergil; but the list of sins in our Apocalypse, among which that against "the way of righteousness" or "the way of God" stands out conspicuously, has its parallel only in the second book of the Sibyllines, and is decidedly Jewish in character. This is confirmed by the Apocalypse ascribed to Joshua ben Levi of the third century, as we shall see in our next chapter.

Quite different is the Apocalypse of Paul,[4] which first appeared at the close of the fourth century, with the claim of having been found, owing to an especial revelation, in the apostle's house in Tarsus. It made such an impression upon the following centuries that for some time it was read in the Church like any New Testament book and was circulated in many translations in the Syriac and Latin, as well as modern languages, so as to become a popular book. It is probably referred to by Dante in his Inferno ii, 31, when he speaks

---

[4] See Tischendorf, "Apocalypses Apocrypha"; James' "Visio Pauli"; Brandes' "Visio Pauli," Halle, 1885; and Robinson, "Texts and Studies," II, Cambridge, 1893.

of Paul as "the chosen vessel who travelled to those regions beyond." The compilatory character of the Apocalypse has been generally recognized by the critics, but the state of disorder and confusion in which the more favored second part is found, dealing with the description of hell and its punishments, shows the many alterations, interpolations, and dislocations which portions of it have undergone in the course of centuries at the hands of medieval monks and ecclesiastics.

As the beginning shows, it is based upon Paul's saying in II Corinthians xii, 9, that "he was caught up to the third heaven where he heard unspeakable words which it is not lawful for man to utter." Still it is noteworthy that no trace of Paul's doctrines concerning salvation by grace and original sin caused by the first Adam and to be atoned by the voluntary death of Christ as the new Adam, is found throughout the Apocalypse, though later ecclesiastical views have been inserted. The main part of the Apocalypse lays all stress on repentance, for the preaching of which the apostle is, like Enoch and Abraham in the Jewish Apocalypses, sent forth by God through the vision he receives. So are the modes of reward of the righteous and of punishment of the wicked originally conceived in the spirit of pure ethics, while only the narrow ecclesiasticism of the Middle Ages confounded the system by its interpolations. Omitting the introductory paragraphs which relate to the finding of the Apocalypse, we notice a twofold address of the apostle at the bidding of the Lord, one to "the children of Abraham who are doing Satan's work" and another to "the sons of men whose sinful nature provokes the wrath of God." This is followed by a dramatic appeal of sun, moon, stars, and the earth to God to bid them destroy the iniquitous race which commits adultery, fornication, murder, theft, violence, and sorcery, but to each God replies: "My eyes behold and My ears hear it all; and nothing is hidden from Me, but My goodness and long-suffering bear with them; peradventure they may turn and repent, and their sins be forgiven. If they do not repent and turn to Me, I shall judge them with a righteous judgment, and shall reward every man according to his deeds." Also when the angelic spirits of men, who give God account of their doings each day, complain of their wickedness and their neglect to pray for the divine forgiveness, God says to them: "Cease not to serve them as their guardian angels; peradventure they may repent and turn to Me before I judge them with a righteous judgment." The absence even of the name of Christ in this highly poetic portion is certainly most significant.

The real vision begins with paragraph eleven, describing the place of the righteous and their departure from earth, and then the place of the wicked and their departure. The latter are seen surrounded by the powers of this world, the spirits of deception, of accusation, of lewdness, and of avarice, and "angels in whom there is no mercy are sent for the souls of those sinners who do not repent, nor believe in God and wait for His salvation." The former were led by angels of righteousness, with faces bright as the sun and girdles of gold and pearls, holding in their hands crowns, and having the name of the living God inscribed on them.

(Here the Latin version has the Son of God instead.) They were to carry these righteous souls in meekness before the throne of God. On looking down upon the tiny earth beneath, the apostle saw first a fiery cloud spread over the whole world, being told that this was the iniquity coupled with the perdition of the sinners.

He then beheld a righteous man at the point of death when all his good deeds stood by him as his angels, promising him a place among the saints at the Resurrection, whereas the bad angels, with all the wicked powers under heaven, the spirits of deception, of temptation, and of lust, fought in vain for the possession of his soul. Amidst the praises of all the angels and the prayers of his guardian angel, his soul is, then, at the bidding of the heavenly voice, committed to the archangel, Michael, the doorkeeper of Paradise, there to be kept until the day of Resurrection. At this sight the myriads of adoring angels and archangels, the cherubim and seraphim, and also the twenty-four Elders we know from the Book of Revelation shout forth: "Just art Thou, O Lord, and righteous are Thy judgments" (Ps. cxix, 1, 37). Seeing on the other hand the wicked man depart from life, which was nothing to him but eating and drinking—(Here a sentence is inserted which refers to the descent of Christ to Hades and which had no place in the original)—the apostle finds him in the last hour embittered by the aspect of all the wickedness he had committed, so that he cries out: "It would have been better for me if I had not been born!" and all the good angels flee away from him, and even his own guardian spirit turns away in distress at his lifelong refusal to repent. And in answer to all the appeals made to God for his forgiveness, the Heavenly Voice is heard, saying: "Whosoever hath shown mercy, mercy will be shown to him, but he who hath shown none, will not be dealt with mercifully, either. So let this soul be delivered to the relentless *Temeluchos*, the keeper of the place of torment, and be cast into outer darkness where there is but wailing and gnashing of teeth." At these words the voices of the myriads of angels are echoed forth: "Thou, O Lord, are just, and righteous is Thy Judgment!"

But then one soul was heard in its dire suffering saying: "I have not sinned, O Lord!" when the great Judge of heaven summoned the angel who kept account of men's doings to come forth with his writing, and he said: "Behold, such are the sins committed by this soul from his *fourteenth* year until this day!" whereupon the Heavenly Voice was heard saying: "If thou hadst repented but three days before now, not one of thy sins would have been remembered. And now I swear by My angels and the strength of My arm, if thou hadst repented but one hour before thy death, I would have received thee." Then all the souls against whom this person had sinned stood up as witnesses against him; one person whom he had killed, another with whom he had committed adultery, and likewise the children that had become victims of abortion, and forthwith the lying soul was handed over to Tartaruchos, the keeper of the lowest hell, while the myriads of angels uttered, as before, their praise of God's justice.

After this the apostle was carried to the third heaven

(Ch. xix ff.) and shown the golden gate of the city of God, through which only the simple-minded and pure of heart are permitted to enter (Ps. cxviii, 20). There he saw two golden tables covered with writings containing the names of the righteous. At the opening of the gate a man of angelic appearance saluted him with a kiss, yet his sad countenance told of his deep sorrow at men's ingratitude toward their Maker, whose commandments they failed to obey. This was Enoch, "the scribe of righteousness." Then Elijah came and saluted him, also complaining that so few of mankind are admitted to these places there. As he proceeded, the apostle was told by his angelic guide not to reveal the mysteries of the place to any living man. From the topmost heaven, where the throne of God's glory was assumed to be, the apostle goes down to the second heaven, and there he beholds the heavenly river, with myriads of gigantic trees on both sides, bringing forth every month fruits of many kinds (= Ezek. xlvii, 12), and the tree of life in the midst of this luminous and most desirable creation of the living God. At the same time he is told, that "seven times more delightful places are prepared for the righteous," "things which eye hath not seen, nor ear heard" (Is. lxiv, 3). Thus a land brighter than silver and gold with wondrous produce is promised to the meek and chaste; and here in the Christian spirit are added "those that preserve their virginity," being celibates. A golden ship upon the wondrous oceanic river—called after the Sibylline Books the Acherusian Lake, for which the Syrian version has the Sea of Eucharist—brings him to the city of God, the celestial Jerusalem—named here the city of Christ—with its twelve gates and twelve walls, illumined by a light seven times as bright as the sun. Like the biblical Garden of Eden, it has at its four sides four rivers, one flowing with honey and called Phishon, the other with milk and called Euphrates, the third with oil, Gihon, and the fourth with wine, Tigris. Upon the river of honey was the city of the prophets, and there the apostle was greeted by each of the prophets from Moses to Zachariah and the rest. At the river of milk at the South he beheld the guileless infants (the insertion, "Whom Herod slew," only betrays the hand of a naïve New Testament reader), and he was told that here was the dwelling place of the pure and childlike. On the river of wine in the North he saw the residences of the venerable fathers of yore, the patriarchs, and Job, and was told that those who love the stranger and show kindness to their fellow-men are to be in this company. On the river of oil in the East there were those who had consecrated their lives to God. (Here follows a paragraph assigning a special place of honor to such as are ignorant and without books, and in their simplicity, while lowly and despised, continually commune with God. It needs little argument to show that this is an insertion of some Christian recluse.) In the midst of the celestial city, King David, with a face shining like the firmament, was seen standing near a high altar, playing the harp and the cither and singing Hallelujah, in which the whole city chimes with reverberating shouts of Hallelujah. (Here an interpolator makes reference to Christ, and this is followed by an odd interpretation of the term Hallelujah with some corrupt Aramaic words, and an admonition to Church-goers not to neglect to respond to the songs and prayers of the service.) Before entering the city, the apostle tells that he saw in front of the gate great and very high trees, having only leaves, but no fruits, and under these trees there were a few men weeping whenever some righteous man entered the city, and he was told, "The root of all evil is false pride," and like these trees barren of fruit, were these men, haughty while fasting and praying, but lacking the fruit of righteousness, humility, and regard for others. Only when they have put aside their conceit will they be admitted at the coming of the Lord of Glory. (Christ is an addition.)

From there (Ch. 31) he was led to the Western end of heaven where the great ocean surrounds the earth, to see the place of torment of the sinners, where there, prevailed only darkness, mourning and groaning. There he beheld a river of fire—the Periphlegeton of the Greeks—in which men and women stood sunk to their knees, others to the navel or belly, and again others to their lips and eyelids—some versions read also, "to the arms and ears"—to suffer for the sins committed by the one or the other member of their body. But the real order of these sins, as it was undoubtedly given in the original, has not been preserved in the various versions. Mentioned are only the blasphemers and slanderers who sin with their lips, the murderers, infanticides, and abortionists whose sins point to the belly, the thieves who sin with their arms, and the usurers and betrayers of the poor, the orphans and widows, and niggards whose evil eye is the source of their sins. The medieval ecclesiastics and monks, however, were apparently not satisfied with the chastisement of sins against morality or against God and religion in general, but wanted to have whisperers during the service, faithless priests, bishops, deacons, and readers of the Church, and especially disbelievers in the dogmas of the Church, singled out for severe and gruesome punishment, and their narrow-mindedness appealed most to the readers or hearers. Hence the diversity and disorder throughout the entire portion.

Especially significant is the fact that there is mentioned a class of men who "were not on a level with the righteous nor with the wicked, but filled up their life in error, serving their body and indulging in evil imaginations, failing to repent," in other words, the intermediate class of the Parsee and the Jewish Eschatology, but what was their fate is no longer stated, because the copyists no longer understood the meaning of the text.

Brought to another river of fire of immense depth the bottom of which could not be reached within a hundred years, the apostle saw it filled with numerous souls whose torment was such as to cause him to weep; but his angelic guide reproached him saying: "Wherefore dost thou weep? Art thou more merciful than God?" Whereupon he humbly acknowledged his weakness, asserting his belief in God's goodness and long-suffering unto the sons of men. (Again it is to be noted that not a word is mentioned concerning Christ's mediatorship.)

A third river of fire showed men and women tortured by "the worm that dies not" (Is. lxvi, 24) and dragons—some versions have here Behemoth (and Leviathan)—who opened their mouths ever anew to devour them.   There were seen usurers and despisers of the word of God gnawing at their tongues.   A pit filled with blood held sorcerers, adulterers, oppressors of widows and orphans, unchaste women clad in black garments, and mothers against whom their slain children cried out for revenge.   But when their ghastly torments moved the apostle to more tears of compassion, the angel told him that he has not seen real pain as yet, and he led him to a pit closed with seven seals, at the opening of which there came out an unbearable stench. It contained seven plagues for seven types of sin.   There were those that were continually cast from coals of fire to piles of snow and ice and back again, and they cried forth, "Oh, that we would never have been born!"   The sin they were guilty of was that they said there is no Resurrection; but the present text has all kinds of disbelief in the Christian dogma instead!

Here follows a touching scene.   The unfortunate sinners, on seeing the apostle and his angelic guide weep, cried forth: "O Lord God, have mercy upon us!"   And there behold, the archangel Gabriel with the whole host of angels came down from heaven, all joining in their supplications, saying: "O Lord God, have mercy on the work of Thine hand.   Have mercy on Thine image!" Then the very heavens shook like trees before the wind, and the twenty-four Elders cast themselves down before God, making supplication in the sight of the altar, the veil, and the throne of glory.   And there, amidst the sound of the trumpet, the Son of God came down in all his glory and said, "What do My glorious angels desire?" and they answered and said, "Plenitude of Thy mercy for the sons of men!" And all the tormented souls cried aloud, "Son of God, have mercy upon us!" Whereupon a voice was heard saying: "What good have you done that you should deserve respite? You have but followed your own desire, and did not repent, spending your life in licentiousness. Still for the sake of Gabriel, the angel of righteousness, and of Paul my beloved, I grant you the night and the day of Sunday, the day of my resurrection, for respite." And forthwith all the tormented broke forth into a cry of thanksgiving and said, "This very respite is better than the whole life we passed in the world above." This beautiful episode casts a flood of light upon the whole Apocalypse. While it became the favorite thought of the Middle Ages—inasmuch as it was a welcome antidote to the belief in the eternity of the torments of hell, and lent a certain cheerfulness to Sunday as the day of the resurrection of Christ—its origin is to be found in the older Jewish belief, as found in the Talmudic and Midrashic sources. It says there: "Every Friday, at nightfall, Dumah, the angel set over the dead in 'the land of Silence,' calls out to the dwellers in hell, 'Let the wicked here have their Sabbath rest!' and when the Sabbath closes with nightfall the following day, he again calls out, 'Return to your torment in Gehenna,' as the people of Israel have finished their Sabbath service!" The underlying idea is that the Sabbath rest, being implanted in creation by God, is observed in hell and heaven as well as on earth. But a critical examination

of the whole Apocalypse shows that just as the idea of
a Sabbath rest for the unfortunate in hell has been taken
over by the Christian Apocalyptist and given its Christian character, so some of the principal ideas of the
whole Apocalypse, such as the vindication and glorifica-
tion of God's justice in the sight of affliction even in hell,
and the joyous salutation or wailing of the angels at
their meeting the souls of either the righteous or the
sinners on their departure from life, have been simply
taken over from the Jewish, or Essenic sources, and only
superficially transformed for the Christian reader.[5]
As a matter of fact, however, these eschatological ideas
can all be traced back to Parseeism.

Here the original Apocalypse apparently ended.
The following seven paragraphs are a repetition of the
former portion of Paradise taken from another version
in which the order of succession of Paradise and Hell is
reversed, and which shows a strong anti-Jewish bias,
while the whole ends abruptly. Its pronounced Christian character is shown in the more elaborate description of the tree of life where the Holy Ghost rested, and
the tree of knowledge of good and evil through which
Adam and Eve sinned, bringing thereby death into the
world. Near the tree of life guarded by the cherubim
and the fiery sword, Mary, the mother of Jesus, appears

---

[5] See Sanh. 65b; Gen. R. xi, 6; Jellinek. B. H. I. 74; 184 and for the
rest see Isr. Levi in Revue des Etudes Juives xxv, 1-13; also in regard to the other views of the Apocalypse expressed in far older
Jewish sources see especially Sifre to Deut. xxxii, 4; Ab. Zara 18a
and Joshua ben Levi in Erubin 19a; Keth. 104a; Eccl. R. to i, 15;
Sota 3b; also Testament Asser. 6; Test. Naphtali 8 and Revelation
xiv, 13. As to the Parsee views see Boecklen, "D. Verwandschaft d.
jŭdishen, christlichen und parsischen Eschatologie," pp. 40-50.

to the apostle, praising him for his work of salvation for the world through his Church. Then the three patriarchs and afterward the twelve sons of Jacob appear, all lauding him for his preaching and his great labor for the faith in Christ, especially Joseph, referring to his own trial, brought on him by his own brethren. They are followed by Moses, the lawgiver, who, oddly enough, weeps, accusing his own people not merely of idol worship, but also of having committed the cruelty of crucifying the Son of God, and in this condemnation of the crucifiers the patriarchs, as well as all the angels, join, asking for their immediate destruction, while God alone restrains them. The prophets, twelve in number, also appear: Isaiah, Jeremiah, and Ezekiel, each charging his own people with the crime of having slain them, and blessing Paul and those who have been taught by him to believe in Jesus Christ. Lot follows, who is lauded for his hospitality to strangers; then Job, who bravely stood the great ordeal of suffering and also *Satan's* (not his wife's) tempting words: "Curse thy God and die!" and afterward Noah, who had preached repentance to his generation and ceased not praying for them, but in vain. Finally, Enoch and Elias stepped forth as preachers of repentance, but Enoch's address to the apostle is not given in this fragment, with which the Apocalypse closes.

It is difficult to say whether Dante made any direct use of this Apocalypse of Paul, which was utilized by so many visionary monks of the Middle Ages in their descriptions of hell and heaven. This, however, must be stated, that the genius of the great medieval poet would not allow him to indulge in the hatred of the Jews that inspired the writer of the Apocalypse. He voiced the pure sentiments of justice and human ethics, making his Inferno the dispenser and instrument of rigid and impartial justice, and assigning to his Purgatorio the function of administering mercy.

CHAPTER VII

A. *Rabbinic Literature*

Familiarity with the Bible and the classics is generally
regarded as an indispensable factor of intellectual culture, but even among the learned there prevail the
quaintest notions about the character and contents of
rabbinic literature. Few are aware of its close relation
to the New Testament. The Jewish sages and scribes
of old held the key to the faith preached by the apostles
and their followers throughout the West, and to the one
spread, with the aid of the sword, over the other half
of the world by the followers of Mohammed, a faith en-
riched by the philosophy of Greece as well as by the
wisdom of Babylonia and Persia. Scattered over the
lands without possessing a land of their own, the Jews,
during the Middle Ages, carried with one hand the mer-
chandise of the world, and with the other the torch of
knowledge to enlighten the Church Fathers, the priests
and monks, and at the same time to furnish the people
of the Occident with most of the fables and folklore of
the Orient. Thus socially and intellectually the Jews
were factors of our modern civilization. And yet you
can almost count on your fingers the non-Jews who feel

the desire even to glance at the power house of the medieval intellect and the storehouse of multifarious wisdom, such as is presented in the Talmudic and rabbinic lore. It was, indeed, the armory which furnished the Jews with ammunition for the defense of their truth and, at the same time, the battleground for their mental athletics in the decision of the Law; now a granary replete with the precious products of many soils, and then a garden fragrant with the perfume of exotic plants, and again a deep sea waiting for the skilled diver to bring forth rare pearls of wisdom and ethical maxims. Here are treasured up ideas and concepts, transmitted from of old by way of mouth or pen, which have found their echo in Christian and Islamic writings and still cast a flood of light on the meaning and origin of many sayings contained in these.

This is especially the case with the eschatological material with which we are here concerned.[1] Under the name of the Mysteries of Creation, and of the heavenly Throne Chariot of Ezekiel, as well as of the hereafter, the saintly mystics known as Essenes communicated to the few initiated in their esoteric circle what they saw in their ecstatic visions, and what was first the secret lore of the Apocalyptists became, at the decline of their order the property of a larger class of Rabbis. Only occasionally we get glimpses of these ecstatic visions in stories told in the Talmud, after the destruction of the Temple, about the two famous disciples of Hillel, the head of the Jerusalem academy, Jonathan ben Uzziel,

---

[1] See art. "Eschatology" in the Jewish Encyclopedia and in the Dict. of Religion and Ethics; also Bousset, "Die Religion des Judenthums," 2d ed.

the Targumic translator of the Prophets, and Johanan ben Zakkai, the head of the school of Jamnia, and his pupils. As legend would have it, flames issued forth from their mouths, enveloping their bodies as with the fire of Sinai when they revealed the heavenly mysteries to their elect hearers (Sukkah 28ª; Hagigah 14ᵇ). So we are told of the high priest, Jishmael ben Elisha of the same period that, when offering incense in the Holy of Holies, he beheld the majesty of God with the crown-bearing angel, Akathriel, behind Him, and he heard the prayer, "May the attribute of My mercy prevail over that of My justice in favor of My children!" Likewise, we read of four sages of the second century, Ben Zoma, Ben Azzai, Elisha ben Abuyah, and Akiba that, by power of vision, "they entered Paradise," but the first three were dazed and distracted by what they saw, and only Akiba emerged sane and strong in mind and body. (Hag. eodem.) Then there was the famous mystic, Simon ben Yohai, a pupil of Akiba, who is reported as having said, "I looked, and behold, I found but few of the mortals privileged to rise to the upper spheres" (Succ. 44ᵇ, Yer. Ber. 13ᵈ). In the next generation the outstanding figure in mystic lore was Joshua ben Levi, who, while still associated with the Essenes, made eschatology a specialty of his, and whose visions took, as we shall see farther on, an apocalyptic form. A son of his had fallen in his illness into a trance, and on his recovery he said to his father in reply to his question, "I saw a world reversed; those on high were here below, and those below here were on high there"; whereupon Joshua ben Levi remarked, "Thou hast seen the better world" (Pesah. 50^b). A similar saying is ascribed to Jesus, when speaking of the time of the regeneration when the Son of Man shall sit on the throne of His glory with the twelve judges for the twelve tribes of Israel, "Then many shall be the last that are the first, and first that are last" (Matt. xix, 30).

Already in the first century we find the schools of Hillel and Shammai discussing the subject of punishment in the hereafter, and to Daniel's (xii, 2) two classes of men, the righteous to enter everlasting life and the wicked to go to everlasting doom, were added, as the third, those whose merits and demerits are found to be even, when weighed in the balance. The more rigid Shammaites, referring to Zechariah xiii, 9, say that for twelve months they shall have to undergo a purgatory process in the fire of Gehenna, until they are sufficiently cleansed from sin to be admitted into Paradise, whereas the Hillelites reject the idea of a purgatory and, referring to Psalm cxvi, maintain that "He who is abundant in mercy will turn the scales toward mercy" (Tos. Sanh. xiii, 3; R. H. 16^b). This diversity of views of the two schools may be traced through the various Talmudic and apocalyptic sources. So is man's life in general viewed by the former from a more pessimistic standpoint to make them declare that it were better for sinful man not to have been born, whereas the more optimistic Hillelites say, "It is well for man with his mastery over himself to have been born" (Erubin 13^b). A comparison of the Ezra and the Baruch Apocalypse, or of the Book of Jubilees, with the Testaments of the Twelve Patriarchs, shows exactly the same divergence of views, not to mention the New Testament writings. The same difference of principles induced, on the one hand, the rigorous Shammaite, Eliezer ben Hyrcanos, to consign the heathen nations to Gehenna, and the liberal Hillelite, Joshua ben Hananiah, on the other hand, to declare that the righteous among the heathen have a share in the world to come, both basing their views on Psalm ix, 18: "The wicked shall return to Sheol, all the nations that forget God." Eliezer b. H. finds in these words the condemnation of all the heathen nations; Joshua b. H., whose opinion became the generally adopted one, finds in the latter part of the verse the exemption of such as have not forgotten God (Tos. Sanh. xiii, 2). And this very difference of view may be discerned in the apocalyptic, the Talmudic, and the New Testament literature. Moreover, it influenced also the views concerning the relation of the Messiah and the Messianic kingdom to the heathen world, and hence we see the sources vary between nationalism and universalism. As long as the expected resurrection was confined, as in Daniel xii, 2, to the righteous of Israel and then extended to all Israel (Sanh. x, 1, after Is. lx. 21, "Thy people shall all be righteous and inherit the land forever"), it was connected with the Holy Land, called "the land of the living," that is "where the dead will come to life anew," the very name ascribed to the Messiah *Yinnon* (Ps. lxxii, 17) being taken as "the Awakener" (Sanh. 98^b; Pirk. d. R. E. xxxiv, comp. I Thess. iv, 14 f). Later on the resurrection was believed to be universal and to be brought about by the regeneration of the world following the

Messianic era, the last judgment presided over by God himself being the one which would decide the fate of all, as to whether they should enter life eternal or be doomed forever (Sanh. 91^b). Accordingly, Gehenna and Paradise were believed from the very beginning of creation to be the destination of either the God-defying heathen as *the* wicked ones or of Israel as the righteous, God-worshiping people. The ordinary sinners of Israel, for whom Gehenna would be but a purgatory, were to be taken up by Abraham and received into his bosom, that is for admission into Paradise (comp. Erubin 19^a with Luke xvi, 22, and Matt. iii, 9), exactly as Jesus was believed to have descended into Hades to redeem the souls imprisoned there. Suggested by Isaiah lxvi, 23, was the assumption that the torments of hell lasted twelve months, after which the souls of the unredeemed wicked were to be consumed in the fire of Gehenna to become "ashes under the soles of the feet of the righteous" (Mal. iii, 21). As to extraordinary sinners, such as traitors, heretics, and seducers of many, "their worm shall not die, neither shall their fire be quenched" (Is. lxvi, 24; Eduyoth ii, 10; Tos. Sanh. xiii, 4-5). There is, however, throughout the rabbinical literature, echoed forth also by the Apocalyptists, the principle voiced that, inasmuch as man would not endure, if measured by the standard of stern justice, God combined mercy with justice when he created man (Gen. R. viii, 4-8; xii, 15; Midr. Ps. lxxxix, 3). He, therefore, provided from the very beginning, alongside of Gehenna and Paradise, the power of repentance to enable man to escape the former and inherit the latter

(Pesah. 54ᵃ; Midr. Ps. xc, 3; Pirk. d. R. El. iii and xliii). Thus it will be the chief function of Elijah to lead Israel to repentance before the coming of the great Day of Judgment (Mal. iii, 24).

As the main feature of rabbinical literature, it is well to observe that the eschatological views, whether taken over from Parseeism or developed independently by the Apocalyptists, were as a rule based, like other doctrines, upon Scripture interpretation rather than upon mere vision or inspiration. Thus the fundamental Pharisean doctrine of resurrection is based both in the Talmud (Sanh. 90ᵇ) and in the Gospel (Matt. xxii, 92) on the Pentateuchal words "the God of the fathers," only applied differently by the one and the other. Not to mention the argument taken from the grain of wheat rising in a new garb from the soil, found alike in the Talmud there and in the Epistle to the Corinthians xv, 37, it is interesting to find the exquisite parable of the lame and the blind both in the Talmud (Sanh. 91ᵃ) and in the apocryphical book of Ezekiel referred to in early Christian writings. In the former the Psalm (Verse 1, 4), "He calleth to the heaven above, and to the earth that He may judge His people," is applied to the heavenly soul and the earthly body in a dialogue of Judah, the prince and the Emperor Antoninus (Severus), the former telling the story of a king who had set up two guardians for his garden, one of whom was lame and the other blind, yet on returning found the garden robbed of its fruits. When called to account, the one, to exonerate himself, said, "How could I have taken the fruit, being unable to walk?" and the other said, "I am blind; how could I see the fruit on the trees?", but the king placed the lame on the blind man's back, saying, "You both committed the wrong, acting as I showed you." In like manner God will bring the soul and the body together at the resurrection as they were joined in life, and punish them on the great Judgment Day. Similarly were the seven hells and heavens of the Apocalyptists based by the Rabbis on scriptural texts. For Gehenna, Joshua ben Levi found seven biblical names: Sheol, Abaddon, Pit of Corruption, Pit of Horror, Mire of Clay, Shadow of Death, and the Nether Parts of the Earth; according to another version: "The Land of Forgetting" or "of Silence," instead of the one or the other of these. For the seven heavenly mansions of Paradise, Simeon ben Yohai finds "Sevenfold Joy is before Thy face" instead of "abundance of joy" predicated in Psalm xvi, 11, and accordingly seven classes of righteous are pointed out: Such as shine like the sun (Judg. v, 31; Matt. xiii, 43), or, like the moon (Song of Songs vi, 10), or like the stars; others, like the firmament (Dan. xii, 3), like the lightnings, or the torches (Nahum ii, 5), like the lilies (Ps. xli, 1), and like the golden candlestick (Zach. iv, 3). Similarly Paul, speaking of the celestial bodies of men, says (Corinth. xv, 41): "There is one glory of the sun, and another of the moon, and another of the stars. So is the Resurrection of the dead." A more popular eudemonistic view of bliss was based on Isaiah lxv, 13, and Psalm xxiii, 5, where the "eating and drinking of the servants of God" and "the table prepared" for the beloved of God are spoken of. This led to the belief in a Messianic banquet (Aboth iii, 16; iv, 21, comp. Enoch lxii, 14), alluded to by Jesus (Matt. viii, 11; xxvi, 29; Luke xiii, 28 f; xxii, 30), and referred to in Revelation xix, 9, as the Messianic wedding feast, which is based on Isaiah lxii, 5, and xlviii, 12 (Comp. Cant. R. to Song of Songs iii, 21; Pes. R. xli with Matt. ix, 15; xxv, 1 f.). In rabbinic literature it is called the banquet of Leviathan, based on Job xl, 30, which is interpreted, "The companies of the saints shall hold their meal upon it" (B. B. 74^b). Like the Parsee food of immortality furnished by the primeval ox, the leviathan, together with the behemoth of Job, the one a sea monster, the other a land monster, to which was added a gigantic bird found in Psalms l, 11, were believed to supply the menu for the Messianic feast. (See Enoch lx, 7; Baruch Apoc. xxix, 4; Ezra Apoc. vi, 52; Tanh. Beshallah at the close; Midr. to Ps. xviii, 25; xx, 5.) Nor was the wine missing at the table (Matt. xxvi, 29; Ber. 34^b comp. Eccl. ix, 7, which verse was also referred to the hereafter). Against this sensual view Rab, the Babylonian sage of the third century, declared that there is neither eating and drinking nor marrying in the world to come, but the righteous are to be in spiritual communion with God, as were the chosen ones of Israel in Exodus xxiv, 11, who "saw God's glory, and this was their eating and drinking" (Ber. 17^b). R. Johanan, his Palestinean contemporary, differentiates the Messianic age, which is earthly, from the world to come, about which it is said, "Eye hath not seen, nor ear heard, but God alone knows what He hath prepared for him that waits for Him" (Is. lxiv, 3; Ber. 34^b).

About the length of the Messianic age the opinions differ; some make it a millennium, after Psalm xc, 4, or seven thousand years; others four hundred years, after Genesis xv, 13, and Psalm xc, 15, as the Ezra Apocalypse vii, 28, has it; others again only forty years or three generations after Psalm lxxii, 5. (See Sanh. 99^a and the Midr. to the various Psalm passages.)

The beautiful idea, expressed also in the Apocalypses of Peter and Paul, that the sinners in hell are released from pain when they acknowledge the righteousness of the Divine Judgment while joining in the praise of God by the righteous, Joshua ben Levi finds in Psalm lxxxiv, 7, which is interpreted, "They that, having trespassed the will of God dwell in the valley of weeping, which is Gehenna, make it a well of tears to quench its fire, and their praises rise to Him who decideth the judg-ment" (Erub. 19^a, Targum and Midr. ad Locum; Exod. R. vii, 4). So is the striking description in Parsee writ-ings of the beautiful maiden who meets the righteous at his departure from earth as the personification of his virtue to fill him with delight, and of the ugly maiden who meets the sinner as the personification of his guilt to horrify him, paralleled by the rabbinical saying that the righteous will be hailed by groups of good angels, calling out, "He entereth in peace!" "They rest in their place of repose;" "He walketh forward to his goal" (Is. lvii, 2); and the sinners will be met by three groups of chastising angels who call out, "There is no peace to the wicked" (Is. xlvii, 27, and so forth). Others refer to Isaïah lviii, 8, "Thy righteousness shall go before thee"; and *vice versa* to Job vi, 18, "They are

entangled by the paths of their ways, and go into desolation and perish" (Sota 10ᵃ).

All these instances illustrate the rabbinical method of
applying scriptural passages to the accepted eschatological views, and this was followed also by the gospel
writers, especially Matthew, in the endeavor to find sup-
port for the claim of the Messiahship of Jesus. Even
in the story of the Temptation of Jesus by Satan, Scripture passages are quoted by both, as if it had been a
dispute between two schoolmen. Still there is an essen-
tial difference between the rabbinic eschatology and that
of the New Testament, in that the latter has been fas-
tened into a firm, dogmatic creed, allowing no dissension,
whereas the former was regarded simply as the free
expression of individuals allowing for a wide diversity
of opinion. Boldly, therefore, could a Talmudic teacher
of the third century declare, "There will be no Gehenna
in the world to come, but God shall bring forth the sun
from its sheath and cause it to shed forth its burning
rays, which will serve as means of chastisement for the
sinners and offer healing and delight to the righteous
in accordance with Malachi iii, 18 ff" (Ab. Zara 3ᵇ;
Ned. 8ᵇ). Rabbi Hillel, a descendant of the great Hillel
of the fourth century, had the audacity to say, "Israel
needs not look for the advent of the Messiah, since
Isaiah's prophecy about him was already fulfilled in
King Hezekiah" (Sanh. 98ᵇ). And was ever a more
daring remark made by a stanch believer in Scripture
than was that of R. Jose, the pupil of Akiba: "Never
did God's majesty come down to earth, nor did any
mortal, even Moses and Elijah, actually rise up to

heaven, for it says, 'The heavens are the heavens of the Lord, and the earth hath He given to the children of men.'" (Ps. cxv, 16—Sukkah 5ª.)   He obviously deprecated all mystic speculation.

Still mysticism had its way and was fostered more and more, as the sober reasoning of the schools declined. Eschatology became again a matter of apocalyptic vision. The leading minds at the close of the Talmudic period down to the rise of Islam indulged in unbridled imagination; and apparitions of Elijah, the prophet, became a matter of frequent experience. It was especially Joshua ben Levi who was made the legendary hero of visions, and frequent intercourse with the prophet, Elijah, was ascribed to him. Nay more. A Talmudic legend (Ketuboth 77ᵇ) tells of his encounter with the angel of death on the walls of Paradise, where he snatched the angel's sword from him, while leaping over the wall in order to find the place destined for him there. Subsequently arose a large literature ascribing to him a visit to Paradise and Gehenna, and an account of what he saw there. He thus became the Jewish Dante.[2]

Speaking in the first person in an Apocalypse ascribed to him, he describes first the two gates of Paradise, made of carbuncle, where sixty million angels keep watch. When a righteous person arrives, they clothe him with eight garments of glory, and place two crowns, one of gold and another of precious stones, upon his head and eight myrtles into his hand; and with

[2] See Bacher, Agada d. Palest. Amoraer 188-194 and Jellinek's Beth ha Midrash, ii, 48-53; iii, 131 f.; 194 f.; v. 43.

the words "Go and eat thy bread in joy!" (Eccl. ix, 7) lead him to a stream surrounded by all kinds of fragrant plants, from which flow rivers, one of oil, another of balsam, a third of wine, and a fourth of honey. Over each of the righteous a canopy is spread according to his merit, and a table of precious stones, while eternal light is everywhere. There are three compartments, one for childhood, the other for youthful manhood, and the third for old age, and, going through the same each day during the three watches, the righteous enjoy the pleasures of each. There are myriads of trees, one more fragrant than the other, and in their midst the tree of life overshadows the whole of Paradise, while seven clouds of glory overhang it.

There are seven compartments for the seven classes of the righteous, the first for martyrs like Akiba; the second for those who died by the accident of drowning (?); the third for the great masters of the law, such as Johanan ben Zakkai and his disciples; the fourth for those covered by the cloud of glory (?); the fifth for the penitent; the sixth for the childlike who proved chaste throughout life; and the seventh for the poor who amidst privation and suffering attended to the Law.

Another version has seven compartments, in the first of which dwell the proselytes, who joined the faith from mere love, and over them is set Obadiah (probably misspelled for Ebed Melek, the Ethiopian); in the second dwell the penitents, with Manasseh, the son of Hezekiah, at their head; in the third the patriarchs and all Israel, including David and Solomon, but not Absalom, Moses and Aaron presiding over them; in the fourth are all the blameless righteous of later times whose life was bitter like the olive tree; in the fifth, through which the river Gihon flows, Joshua ben Levi saw the palatial dwelling of the Messiah in the company of Elijah, and there was weeping all around, as all Israel was anxiously waiting for his coming, and he himself joined in the weeping; in the sixth dwelt those who met an accidental death, not having had the solemn funeral; and in the seventh those who suffer diseases thereby to atone for Israel's sins.

In the corresponding seven compartments of Gehenna Joshua ben Levi saw pits replete with fiery lions and rivers of fire, and each compartment inhabited by ten of the seventy nations of heathendom and presided over by one of seven Jewish rebels such as Absalom, Doeg the Edomite, Korah, Jeroboam, Ahab, Micah, the idolatrous priest of Judges xviii, and Elisha ben Abuyah, the apostate. These, having been included in the covenant of Sinai, were not doomed to suffer with the heathen nations.

Altogether different in character and spirit and of the same universal or human character as the original Apocalypses of Peter and Paul is another description of Hell by Joshua ben Levi, an undoubtedly older one than the one just given here. Therein he tells how the prophet Elijah brought him to the gate of Hell and showed him men hanging by their hair. These were those who let their hair grow to adorn themselves for sin. Others were hanging by their eyelids; they had followed their eyes lustingly; others by their noses;

they had perfumed themselves to sin. Others again by their tongues; they were slanderers. Others by their hands; they had stolen or robbed. Others by their genitals; they had committed adultery. Again others by their feet; they had run to sin. Women who had bared their breasts before men for sin were hung by their breasts. Blasphemers were fed on fiery coal. Such as ate on fast days were forced to eat bitter gall. Sinners with their mouths had to eat fine sand, until their teeth were broken (after Ps. iii, 8). Men who had abused the needy who had asked them for assistance were thrown from fire to snow and from snow to fire. Others were driven from hill to hill like the sheep by the shepherd (Ps. xlv, 15).

A vision ascribed to Moses in a Midrash to Song of Songs ii, 3 [3], describes his voyage under the guidance of the angel (Enoch) Metatron, through the seven compartments of Gehenna, in which the unfortunate ones are likewise hung by their eyes, ears, tongues, feet, or hands for having sinned with the corresponding member of their body, whether against the moral or the ritual laws. Greatly affected by the sight of these horrors, Moses, knowing that the time for repentance had passed for them in entering the sad place, prayed to God for the release of Israel, his people, from the terrible torment, but God said to him, "Moses, My servant, there is no respect of person, nor taking of bribes with Me; whosoever performs good deeds finds his place in Paradise, and whosoever doeth evil, his place is Gehenna," as

[3] Wertheimer, "Bathe Midrashoth," iv, 22.

it says, "I, the Lord, search the heart; I try the reins to give every man according to his ways, according to the fruit of his doings" (Jer. xvii, 10).

From Gehenna Moses entered Paradise, brought there by the archangel, Gabriel, and, under the guidance of the angel, Sampsiel, came first to behold seventy thrones of gold and silver, pearls, and precious stones, among which the one excelling all the rest was that of Abraham; the next, that of Isaac, and the third, that of Jacob. The rest were assigned to the various classes of the saints according to their rank: the first were those who amidst affliction and privation studied the Law; the second, to the blameless; the third, to the penitents; the fourth, to the proselytes of righteousness; the fifth and sixth class consisting of righteous sons of unrighteous men, such as was Abraham, and of unrighteous sons of righteous men who are saved by the merit of their fathers.

Many of these visions belong to the post-Talmudic period, in which the apocalyptic Essenism of the Enoch writings was revived, and the martyrs of the Hadrianic persecution were made legendary heroes, described as ascending the heavens by means of an ethereal shiplike chariot, to behold all the wonders of the heavenly halls and of creation. Thus eschatology became a popular study, so as to exert a great influence even on the Synagogal liturgy, the poets and philosophers of the Middle Ages. Only the Aristotelian school of philosophers such as Crescas and Maimonides had the courage to oppose it, looking upon heaven and hell as symbols, rather than as localities of God's judgment.

B. *Mohammedan Literature*

Mohammed, the founder of the Islamic faith, whose fervent religious zeal won the millions of the Arabic race for Allah, the God of Abraham, was consigned by Dante to the ninth gulf of the Inferno (xxviii, 28 f.), where he is seen with limbs mangled and ripped in two for having split the Christian world by his schism. We have learned to judge him better than could the Middle Ages.[4] However distorted and confused his hearsay acquaintance with the Old and New Testament stories was in his receptive, yet undisciplined mind, however inferior in every respect he was to Moses and Jesus as a prophet claiming to be the last and the seal of the three great prophets, we cannot deny him a place among the foremost movers and molders of the human race. There is a wondrous spiritual power and poetic grandeur in his impassionate appeal to his idolatrous and vicious countrymen to turn to Allah, the omnipotent Ruler of heaven and earth, the sublime and merciful one, and fear His great judgment in the day of reckoning that is sure and quick to come in the hereafter. True, he was not the first among the Arabs to believe in Allah or in resurrection, but, being of a high-strung, nervous temperament and given to hallucinations and visions, he made his "Koran," the book handed him by the angel, Gabriel, as he saw it in his ecstatic state, the mirror of a revelation that still stirs two or three hundred millions of men to the very core by its profound earnestness. In

[4] R. Bosworth Smith, "Mohammed and Mohammedanism"; Palmer's Koran in S. B. E.; George Sales, "The Koran"; Pautz, "Mohammeds Lehre von d. Offenbarung"; Wolf, "Mohammedanische Eschatologie."

spite of his sensuality, which became more pronounced as he grew older, his vivid description of the terrors of Gehenna and the delights of Paradise impresses the readers of the Koran as much as does any other eschatology, if not more so.   In fact, it may be called the *Leitmotif* of his theology, and its main source is rabbinic, with only a few Parsee elements interwoven.   But, as the whole Mohammedan religion remained national, so also was its eschatology, whether in the Koran or in its later development.

As in rabbinic and older sources, Hell has in the Koran (xv, 44) seven gates for the seven compartments, one below the other, and each gloomier than the other. The one on top is for the disobedient among the Muslims, the second for the Jews, the third for the Christians, the fourth for the Sabeans (who also had some book of Revelation), the fifth for the Parsees or Magians, the sixth for the idolaters, and the seventh—and this is quite characteristic!—for the hypocrites (iv, 44).   It is unnecessary to give the names of each compartment. Suffice it to say that Malik (a derivate of Moloch?), the keeper of hell, has his subordinates to carry out the ordinances of the various punishments for the various sinners (xliv, 18).   "For the infidels we have chains and collars and burning fire," says the Koran (lxxvi, 4).   "He who believed not in God and failed to give the poor their bread, shall feed on corruption and sores" (lxix, 36 f.).   The inmates of the Fire will in their burning thirst cry out to the inmates of Paradise, "Pour upon us some water" (vii, 48), exactly as does the rich man in Luke xvi.

Paradise, with Ridwan as its keeper, has likewise seven compartments, each with a different name, all built up of gold and silver and precious stones. There are also the four rivers, one of pure water, instead of the balsam of the Rabbis, the other of milk, the third of wine, and the fourth of honey. To these were later on added streams of various spices to be mixed with the water. Black-eyed maidens of perennial virginity, whether patterned after Persian custom or Parsee writings, play a prominent rôle in the sensuous system of Mohammedan eschatology, alongside of the wives and beautiful youths who serve the faithful sitting under shady trees or reclining on their costly couches in Paradise. Nor should they miss, according to later tradition, the meat of the Jewish Behemoth and the big earth-encircling fish, Leviathan (Sale, p. 78). Between Hell and Paradise there is a partisan wall (vii, 44 f., comp. Eccl. R. vii, 14 and Phædo, 62). Upon it are placed those who, while worshiping God, have not done good works sufficiently to outbalance their evil deeds, the so-called intermediates of the Talmud. They look with envy upon the inmates of Paradise, and seeing the inmates of Hell, they pray that they themselves may be spared the same pain, but at last by divine grace they will be admitted into Paradise. A later doctrine states that the Mohammedan creed, "There is no Allah but Allah, and Mohammed is His prophet," pronounced by the unfortunate in Gehenna, will at the intercession of the prophet release them, and after having bathed in a Lethelike stream, they will be rejuvenated and then admitted into Paradise. Instead of seven there are in later writings eleven classes of sinners pointed out, such as scandal-mongers, liars, unrighteous judges, the proud and insolent, hypocrites, false witnesses, the unchaste, misers, slanderers, usurers, the fraudulent, also those who neglect their prayers or disturb the public worship, while the twelfth class comprises the good and righteous.

The resurrection is said to take place from Jerusalem at the sound of successive trumpet blasts by the angel, Israfil (= Sarafel). A monster called the Spy will then come out of the earth (xxvii, 84) and mark the foreheads of the faithful with the staff of Moses as the white sign of life, and the noses of the evildoers with the signet ring of Solomon, as the black sign for perdition. Then all will be summoned to the temple hill of Jerusalem, as the highest spot of the earth, for judgment, which will take place at the narrow bridge leading from Hell to Paradise. There no intercession shall avail, except that of Jesus and Ezra (xx, 107, and elsewhere). The deeds of men shall be weighed in the scales, and the books containing the records of the faithful, kept in the seventh heaven, and those of the sinners, kept in the lowest part of hell, will be read, the former to be held in the right hand of the faithful, the latter placed in the left hand of the sinners and tied to their neck. Then "shall Paradise and Gehenna be brought down," and the faithful be welcomed by God and His angels with the greeting, "Peace be on you!" while the unbelievers will be ushered into the wretched abode of Hell, there to dwell forever.

Following rabbinical sayings, the Mohammedan sources assign to each person two angels accompanying him through life, the one at his right recording his good deeds, the one at his left his evildoings. At his departure the virtuous sees his good deeds before him in the shape of a beautiful man to fill him with great joy, and the wicked sees his evil doings in the shape of an ugly man to fill him with horror and dismay. This view is, of course, taken over from the Parsees.

Concerning the visions Mohammed speaks of in the Koran as frequent, if not constant, experiences at the beginning of his career as prophet (liii, 2-8, and lxxxi, 19-23), we find them to be, of course, of an ecstatic state such as Paul and Swedenborg must have had. But his followers saw in them actual ascents of the soul to heaven, and they describe his journey through the seven heavens under the guidance of the angel, Gabriel, and through Gehenna as shown to him by Malik, its keeper. In the first heaven he sees Adam who in his survey of all his descendants lauds the righteous and blames the evildoers. In the second he sees Jesus and John the Baptist, in the third, Joseph, in the fourth, Idris—that is, Enoch—in the fifth, Aaron, in the sixth, Moses, and in the seventh, Abraham. But it is especially Mohammed's reference to this night journey from Mecca, "the Sacred Mosque," to the Temple at Jerusalem called by him, "the remote Mosque" (xvii, 1), which was, of course, only a vision or a dream, that gave rise to the belief of the Muslims in the actual voyage of the prophet to heaven on the miraculous Burak—a sort of lightning-like mule.

As a matter of course the history of Islam tells of many visionaries who journeyed like Mohammed through hell and heaven to see the torments of the sinners and the delights of the faithful, as shown by Hammer-Purgstall in his "Geisterlehre der Moslimen." But while the great mass of Moslems believed as staunchly in these crude notions of Gehenna and Paradise as did medieval Christendom, there arose many classes of free-thinkers in opposition to the same, either rejecting them altogether or allegorizing them. (See von Kremer "Gesch. d. herrschenden Ideen des Islam," pp. 278, 305.)

CHAPTER VIII

HELL, HEAVEN, AND PURGATORY IN
MEDIEVAL LITERATURE

The Middle Ages are called the ages of faith, but it would be more correct to call them the ages of credulity, or of blind belief unenlightened by reason and knowledge and lacking altogether originality of thought. Of course, this does not include the Islamic and Jewish world from which the Scholastics received a new impetus to mental endeavor. The masses of Christendom, constituting many races and nationalities, most of them converted to Christianity either by the power of speech or of the sword, were held together by despotism, whether political or hierarchical, and ruled by fear either for the body or for the soul. The Church, in her ascendancy over the State, demanded unreserved submission to her authority upon the condition of future salvation. Education and knowledge, which make men self-reliant, were shunned and suspected, and instead, ignorance and superstition fostered. Tertullian's famous dictum, *Credo quia absurdum*, or more exactly, *Certum est, quia impossible est,* had given the death-blow to reason and independent inquiry. Hence the belief in miracles and ghosts grew like mushrooms in marshy soil. The fear of hell and the devil by far eclipsed the fear of God, and the old pagan deities and demons only helped to increase the hosts of the Evil One, unless they were turned into saints. Yet in the same proportion grew the power of the clergy, the priests, or the monks who invented ever new means of mediation between man and the Deity in the shape of relics or of sacraments. Though learning found here and there shelter in some cloister, the people at large were not affected by it, as they knew no Latin and could not even read the Scripture in the Vulgate. Only art was cultivated, not for art's sake as an expression of beauty, but as reflecting the emotional element, and particularly the passion typified in the crucified Savior and the Mater Dolorosa. It was an appeal to the senses in hallucinations and visions which were believed to indicate the presence of the Divine in opposition to the devil. In like manner did poetry and music culminate in the thrill of awe expressed in *"Dies Irae"* and *"Stabat Mater."* As has well been said,[1] "there was no reliance on sin-crushed self. There was a constant conflict between the heavenly joy of the divine world, symbolized in the Church dome and the fleshly joy of the devil's lures, between the lust and vainglory of the earth and the salvation in the beyond, between life's terror and its pitifulness, and its eternal hope over which flamed the terror of darkness and the Judgment Day." To this corresponded the contrast between the asceticism of monk or nun, of hermit, flagellant or saint, and the unbounded licentiousness of the semi-barbarian mob, or the idealized illicit love of romantic knighthood; like-

---

[1] See H. O. Taylor, "The Medieval Mind," for the whole chapter.

wise between the all-powerful Church with her penances and penitences offering expiation for every sin or crime, however revolting, and an unredeemed heathen world whose very virtues were declared by Augustine, the Church Father, to be only shining vices (Civitas Dei xix, 25). It is, indeed, worth noting that Dante, the greatest genius of the Middle Ages, not merely felt in his soul, but actually experienced in his own life, this raging conflict between the carnal and the spiritual, between the secular and the eternal, seeking its reconciliation in his immortal poem both for his own satisfaction and for that of the Christian believer. Whether he satisfies the modern thinker is a question we shall consider in our next and last chapter. Our purpose here is to follow up the views and visions presented in the medieval literature preceding him.

And here we are struck by the significant fact that the apocalyptic vision of Paul we discussed in Chapter vi, which circulated in ever so many versions throughout the Middle Ages, dwelt more and more upon the description of the terrors of Hell, and of the Purgatory which was inserted later with the emphasis laid on the Sunday respite for the unfortunate, whereas the delights of Paradise were more and more omitted. The reason is obvious. Paradise was regarded as attainable only by the elect few, the real saints whose blameless life was considered as having been angelic. In its place Purgatory loomed up as the realm of hope for those whose overwhelming burden of sins was to be lightened and ultimately removed by the cleansing process of fire, since those "cursed" by the Son of Man, are according to

Matthew xxv, 41, doomed to go "into everlasting fire prepared for the devil and his angels."

Now the idea of the purgatorial function of a middle or temporary state of the sin-laden soul goes back to India and Persia, to Plato and Vergil, and is maintained, as we have seen in the previous chapter, by the Shammaite school as well as in the New Testament. (See Luke xvi, 23, where Hades is not identical with Gehenna.) To secure release for those suffering in this temporary state, prayers and almsgiving were resorted to in Hindu and Persian, as well as in Jewish circles. For the latter II Maccabees xii, 42-45, has become the classic passage, as it has also for early Christian practice. (See also Sifre Deut. 210.) It was, however, only the last of the Church fathers, Gregory the Great of the sixth century, who invested the doctrine of the purgatory with the character of a dogma for the Roman Church, and for which he instituted the mass. Henceforth it became the chief instrument of ecclesiastical power and profit. But strange to say, it was mostly Ireland and England that became its main propagators, foremost among whom was the Venerable Bede of the eighth century, the then acknowledged master of medieval lore. He illustrated the doctrine by the visions of two famous monks, Furseus and Dhrithelm, which, next to the Vision of St. Paul, became very popular and were made the pattern of many others.[2]

Furseus, an Irish monk who built monasteries in Ire-

[2] See for all this Th. Wright, "St. Patrick's Purgatory": "Essay on the Legends of Purgatory"; "Hell and Paradise current during the Middle Ages"; also Baring-Gould, "Curious Myths of the Middle Ages": "St. Patrick's Purgatory," p. 230 ff.

land, England, and France, describes in his vision how in his deathlike sleep he was carried to heaven by angels who sang the Psalm verse, "They go from strength to strength" (Ps. lxxxiii, 8); and then he saw, far beneath, a deep valley full of fierce demons, having four fires at different places, one to burn the lovers of falsehood, the other the avaricious, the third those who stirred up strife and discord, and the fourth the fraudulent and impious. Owing to some slight sin of his, he was scorched by a demon, as he passed, but was lifted up again to heaven, there to behold the saints enjoying the fellowship of the angels.

Dhrithelm beheld the deep and broad valley one half filled with roaring flames, and the other half with storms of hail and snow, between which the unfortunate were tossed to and fro as globes of fire amidst terrible wailing. Yet this was only the Purgatory; the real Hell far below was far more horrible with its darts of fire, the very nearness of which scorched him, too. On the other side, behind a great wall, he beheld numerous people in shining garments enjoying the delights of the place replete with light brighter than sun and moon and fragrant with flowers, and yet this was only the fore-court of Paradise, the dwelling place of such as had done good works on earth, but had not yet attained the per-fection of the saints. These lived in a still brighter realm, resounding with music and song, enjoying the fellowship of Christ and his angels, the real Paradise. This he could only look at from the distance, not being permitted to enter.

A vision ascribed to Charles the Fat of France, of the

ninth or tenth century, indicating the influence of St. Paul's Vision, is interesting only in so far as it consigns to the Purgatory, with its great torments, bishops, barons, and kings for the mischief and wrong caused by them, for which they are punished by having to stand up to their hair or chin or navel in pits of sulphur and burning oil, or water, or in streams of melting metal.

.A vision of Tundale of the twelfth century has the parricides, the fratricides, and the homicides melted in a great iron boiler, the deceitful and treacherous tossed about alternately in fire and ice; the proud cast down from a narrow bridge into a deep, stinking valley; the avaricious devoured by a terrible monster called Acheron (probably originally Leviathan). Thieves are forced to carry their stolen goods over a bridge, with sharp spikes that pierce their feet as they go across—Tundale himself was thus slightly punished for having once stolen a calf.—Monks, nuns, and ecclesiastics who had led an unholy life were devoured by another frightful winged beast and, when ejected, tormented again by serpents. The last he saw there was the Vale of the Smithies in charge of Vulcanus, the Greek god. There the great criminals were beaten to formless mass. But the chief sufferer was—and here we have Dante's prototype—Lucifer, the prince of hell who was tormented by fires kept up by gigantic fiends blowing the bellows with thousands of hands to fan the flames. On passing a great wall he came first to a place where such souls as were neither very good nor very bad suffered from hunger and thirst, waiting to be admitted after a certain time to Paradise. But he was admitted only to the forecourt where those whose sins were expiated lived. Into the glorious dwelling place of the saints behind the other great wall he could not enter.

Matthew of Paris tells of two famous visions at the close of the twelfth century. The one by the monk of Evesham contains nothing new, except that he describes three compartments of hell and correspondingly three compartments of heaven. More interesting is the vision of Thurcill, a hospitable farmer of a village in Essex at the beginning of the thirteenth century, who was taken by St. Julian, his grateful guest, into "the center of the world" and led to a hall whither the souls went on their departure from earth. Near by was the forecourt of Purgatory where slight sins were punished, and the Purgatory in charge of St. Nicholas. From there a great bridge covered with nails and spikes led to the Mountain of Joy. In the reception hall St. Michael, St. Peter, and St. Paul were in attendance. St. Michael led the spotless and perfectly white souls through the flames up to the Mount of Joy, St. Peter led the spotted souls to the Purgatory, and St. Paul had opposite him the Devil, while watching the scales in which the souls were weighed, to have those inclined toward the apostle sent to the Purgatory, the others to the fiery pit, right under the feet of the grinning devil. There proud churchmen, faithless priests, frivolous knights, and bribe-taking lawyers underwent scrutiny in the presence of Thurcill, who was led hence to the earthly Paradise. There he saw Adam—similarly to the Testament of Abraham— laughing with one eye and weeping with the other at the sight of the few who were admitted into Paradise, and the many who had to meet their fate in hell, while Adam himself was stripped of his robe and splendor of immortality, which he recovered in part through Abel, and the other elect ones, but which in their entirety he will recover only at the end of the world, when the virtuous will all gather around him.

The famous St. Patrick's Purgatory, which seems to have originally been one of the many supposed entrances to hell in ancient folklore, had as one of its legendary heroes, Owain, an Irish knight who, according to Matthew of Paris, went there to do penance for his sins. He is said to have gone through four fields of punishments, in the last of which the unfortunate were hung up by the various members of their body with which they had sinned. From an icy lake called the Devil's Mouth, he was led across a beautiful gate to the earthly Paradise, where Adam and Eve had transgressed, to be cast into hell together with Lucifer, until they and their worthy descendants were rescued by Christ's Descent.

It would lead us too far afield, if we would continue taking notice of all these medieval visions, some of which had also Norse and Icelandish sagas interwoven, while French Troubadours of the thirteenth century offered, instead of visions, dreams of hell and Paradise. Of direct influence upon Dante was the Vision of Alberic, monk of Monte Casino at the beginning of the twelfth century, who described what he saw as a child of ten years in a trance after a nine days' and nights' deathlike sleep. Carried up by a white dovelike bird, he meets St. Peter with two angels, and is led first to the Limbus Infantum where little children in proportion to their age are purged; then to the real Purgatory, at which adulterers and other impure souls have to undergo the fire and ice punishment. Elsewhere mothers who refused nurture to their children were seen hung up by their breasts; faithless women by their hair. Severer punishments were inflicted upon tyrants, upon mothers guilty of infanticide, upon persons guilty of sacrilege, simony, slander, false testimony, and theft. On the borders of hell two malignant spirits, in the shape of a dog and a lion, spat fire out of their mouths to prevent escape, and over the fiery river an iron bridge was spanned which appeared broad and easy to pass for the virtuous, but grew narrow as a thread under the feet of the sinners who attempted to pass, to cause them to fall into the boiling pitch beneath. From there a road, covered with thorns and brambles, and watched by a cruel demon, led the souls, after they had passed the test of purification, to a very pleasant fragrant plain filled with joy by the good people, martyrs, and monks. In the midst of this there rose the Mountain of Paradise, with its tree of life. From there he was conducted through the *seven* heavens, the circles of the Moon, the Mars, the Mercurius, the Sun, Jupiter, Venus, and Saturn, where the cherubim surrounded the Throne of Glory. In the sixth heaven he beheld the archangels, the patriarchs, prophets, and apostles, the Virgin, St. Peter, and also St. Benedict, but what he saw behind the wall there of the Empyrean with the Trinity, he was forbidden to tell. Obviously much of the material contained in the rather wearisome forty-five chapters of this Vision of Alberic served Dante as model.

While the substance of these visionary voyages to the other world as developed through the centuries was thus used by our great poet, he took the spirit from the great mystics of the Middle Ages. To understand this spirit, we have to go back to the Church Father, Origen, who beheld in the Song of Songs an allegorical bridal duet between the soul and her bridegroom, Christ, the God-man, as it was originally taken by the Rabbis to be a nuptial song of Israel and God. The very sensuousness of the biblical dialogue of love appealed to the imagination of the Christian mystic, since celibacy was regarded as a higher state than married life, and monk, nun, and priest were to consider themselves as wedded to Christ, the Bridegroom. It is easy to understand how this psychological sex motive worked all the stronger upon the ascetic women in their ecstatic visions. And, strange to say, this love motive, not having justice as corrective and basic principle, led to injustice, to such partiality as to put hatred at the opposite end. Heaven as the realm of love and bliss for the saints had its logical counterpart in Hell as the realm of eternal doom for the wicked and infidels, to be hated like the devil himself. Of Beruria, the gentle-souled wife of Rabbi Meir of the second century, the Talmud relates that, on hearing her famous husband in his indignation at some wicked neighbors pronounce a curse upon them, she said: "Pray, do not curse! Instead of reading in the Psalm verse civ, 35, 'Let the sinners perish from the earth,' you had better read, 'Let the sins cease from the earth,' and the wicked will be no more!" Not so the saints and saintly women of the Middle Ages. With all their love for God and Christ, they turned their hatred of sin to the sinners, and their wrath against the devil to the unbelievers. Thus St. Bernard of Clairvaux, the greatest saint of the Middle Ages—whom Dante places in his Paradiso next to the holy Virgin, his adored Queen of Heaven, and whose speeches and writings, especially his sermons on the Song of Songs, are aglow with the most fervent love for Christ, the ever-yearned-for and ever-yearning Bridegroom of the soul—has but the fiercest utterances of wrath and condemnation for heretics and schismatics, "the enemies of God," to persecute whom was deemed by him the holiest task, as he, indeed, started the second Crusade. This is not the place to point out the striking contrast between those vehement outpourings of mystic love in his exposition of the Song of Songs and those harrowing execrations hurled against dissenters. Nor did the saintly women of the same century remain behind the famous saint in either their mysticism or their fanaticism. More receptive than creative among these was Elizabeth of Shoenau on the Rhine, as she describes her vision of the heaven with the Lamb of God, and "the Queen of Kings and Angels," the radiant Cross at the left of the Trinity, and the twenty-four Elders, all taken from the Apocalypse of John, and likewise her vision of the last days of the Saviour. But she also preached vigorous sermons from scriptural texts, assigning backsliding prelates, monks, and nuns to hell, while the blessed martyrs were seen by her in celestial beatitude. Of greater originality and influence was Hildegard of Bingen on the Rhine, who, in her letters addressed to all the great men of her time as well as in all her writings, spoke as a seeress inspired by "the living light" of God, and exerted like St. Bernard a certain influence, even if only indirectly, on Dante. In her "Book of the Rewards of Life," in which the heavenly love is contrasted with the love of the world, she describes the punishments of the sinners in hell and the delights of the blessed in Paradise. But, as Dante's Inferno is far more dramatic in presenting the passion and strife of the sinner, whereas Paradiso is all mysticism in lyric form, so also are the former given with all the pathos of life and the latter rather in dull and lifeless imagery.

Among the numerous visionary women of this class, all of whom revelled in love for their heavenly Bridegroom or Spouse, using frequently the most sensuous expressions of Sulamit and King Solomon in the Song of Songs, such as "the Couch," Mechthild of Magdeburg and Mechthild of Hageborn must be specially mentioned as being referred to three times in the Purgatorio xxviii, 41; xxxii, 82, and xxxiii, 119, as Mathilda. The former's dithyrambic love for her Lord took its color from the secular love poetry of the time. She is ever ready to die, yearning for a kiss from Him who died on the Cross, and only tears can cool off her fiery passion. The latter hears Jesus address her in words of the Song of Songs; she speaks of the seven steps of ascent to heaven, two thrones, one for Jesus, the other for his Virgin Mother, also of the celestial Rose and other sights presented in the Empyrean.

Reading such outbursts of passionate love, with which Troubadour or minstrel adores the woman of his choice, applied to the ecstasies of mystic love often called forth by the cult of the Madonna, we realize how Dante, who tasted enough of each as Troubadour and as spiritual lover, came to idealize his Beatrice, to be lifted up by her to heaven's sublimest love as the crowning goal of life, while saintly women from Rachel, the beloved wife of Jacob, to Lucia, Italy's martyr saint, led the way. Nor must we omit to mention Hughes and Richard of St. Victor at Paris, who preceded these saints in the apotheosis of love. As a matter of fact, the former also found in women such as Rachel and Leah types of virtue and vessels of the holy spirit, the one as presenting contemplative, the other practical, life. So does the Song of Songs appeal to him to seek rest from the world's unrest in the Bridegroom's arms, and he, too, longs for a kiss from the mouth of the Incarnate Son of God. Still more extravagant in his mystic effusions is his pupil Richard.

It was Dante's good fortune to be drawn out of this torpid atmosphere of emotionalism into the intellectual sphere of stern philosophy by the great master of scholasticism, Thomas Aquinas. Through him the poet was transformed into a theologian and a philosopher familiar with Aristotelian thought as interwoven with Christian doctrine, and thus his love expanded into love for pure truth, for philosophy typified by Vergil, and for theology, the divine science typified by Beatrice. As the new knowledge of the classics and especially of Aristotle streamed into Western Europe, and the works of Mohammedan and Jewish thinkers circulated in Latin translations, the mental horizon of Aquinas and his teacher, Albertus Magnus, expanded, to enable especially the former to concentrate the whole medieval theology and systematize it in his "Summa Theologiæ." So was Dante, the artist, induced to sum up the whole of Christian thought and aspiration in a grand poem which, while presenting the plan of Christian salvation, would mirror all the conflicts and convictions, the experiences and hopes of the medieval world. It is, moreover, an allegorical drama of man, beginning with the tragedy of the damned with all its human pathos, and following with tender sympathy the arduous efforts toward freedom and purification, ending in the triumphant joy of the blessed, which the poet calls the "Divine Comedy." Thus he created out of the depths of his own life with its strifes and struggles the masterpiece of art to be accorded a prominent place among the great teachers of the Church, as was done by the other great Italian artist Raffael in his *Disputa*.

The question, however, whether man after life's toils and struggles is really satisfied with that quietude of rest which is offered in the contemplation of the divine glory by Dante's Paradiso, can be better discussed in our last chapter. The Psalmist's verse, "They go from strength to strength, until God is seen on Zion" (Ps. lxxxiv, 8) has led the Rabbis of old to remark, "The righteous find no real rest either in this world, nor in the world to come, but go from stage to stage onward, until the highest perfection is reached in an ever closer communion with the Deity." In other words, there is no standstill either in earthly life nor in the hereafter. God as the all-encompassing energy of life must of necessity impart His own energizing power throughout time and eternity to man, whose soul will ever thirst after Him as the living God.

CHAPTER IX

THE DIVINE COMEDY IN THE LIGHT OF MODERN THOUGHT

It has well been said that Dante represents the sunset of the Middle Ages. Indeed, as the sun in its setting gilds the Western horizon with all the splendor of its rays to glorify the receding day, so does Dante's masterwork cast its wondrous luster upon the entire medieval world to cover it, together with all its faults and shortcomings, with a mantle of glory. But after all, the new day which was dawning, foreshadowed by the classic Italian vernacular of his swan song, was to part forever with the beliefs and views voiced therein. Contrasted with our cosmic system, our ethical and social concepts of life, and our anthropological and psychological science, and still more with our historical and religious outlook upon life, we look upon the whole of medievalism as a curiosity, as if presented to us in a museum of antiquity. Unless we purposely shut our eyes and ears to the revelations of the modern era since Copernicus and Newton, Kant and Darwin—and there is none so blind as he who will not see, and none so deaf as he who will not hear—Dante's world view is as remote from ours as is the child age from that of mature manhood. It is difficult for us to realize the entire structure of the universe as conceived by the ancient and medieval times, when the vault of heaven with its three or seven stories served as the dwelling place of the Deity with its court of angels or inferior gods around and beneath, and when the corresponding nether world beneath the earth, the abode of men and beasts, with its three or seven chambers was inhabited by the shades of men and the infernal demons. How easily could then a fertile imagination work out a plan for a continuance of the shadowy life of these, either in the dark region below or in the brighter realm in the heavens above, to make it a question of damnation or salvation to be decided by the ruling Church! Surely our enlightened world has outgrown this conception of the cosmos. Our universe with its infinitude of space and time, in which orbs of light without number swing in endless æons through distances far beyond the grasp of the human mind around some unknown center, has no upper nor lower sphere, no celestial or infernal region to localize either the Deity or its counterpart, the devil, with their hosts. In order to find God, while upward looking in our prayer and aspiration, we must needs look *within*, as neither space nor time can encompass Him. And as God has thus become for us both transcendent and immanent, the hosts of angels as well as the demons have ceased to be material entities. Heaven and hell have at best merely symbolic significance, lacking all reality. Geography and history alike compel us to see in the story of Paradise a beautiful parable rather than an actual occurrence, as, in fact, the medieval Jewish philosophers felt it to be.

As we trace life to-day through its various stages,

from the lowest to the highest form, we see man's life to be a constant ascent, and not a fall from grace, unless we ourselves make it thus by our relapse into the state of the brute through passion and guilt. It is man's freedom of will and action which renders him self-conscious and self-determining in contradistinction to the animal below him. Though body and soul are in constant interaction and interrelation with him, as with all living creatures beneath him, he mirrors the Divinity in mind and soul. Scripture, therefore, represents him as made in God's image. At the same time physiology and anthropology forbid us to so separate the soul from the body as to believe that the disembodied spirit of man is after this life to take on again the shape of the body, and, when found guilty on the Judgment Day, to undergo corporal punishments, such as the culprit on earth is liable to, or in case of guiltlessness to enjoy sensuous delights like any mortal man. Hence, while we admire Dante's Inferno as the portraiture of a grand tribunal of justice for the ages of the past, and follow him with reverential awe through his Purgatorio and up to the serene realms of his Paradiso, we must always bear in mind that they have for us only the value of a poetical allegory.

Above all, however, does our ethical view militate against the doctrine of eternal damnation which Dante as a loyal son of the Church accepted, though not without reluctance. The very principle of justice, which he so often accentuates, is violated by the assumption that the sins committed by man during his brief stay on earth should condemn him to endless suffering throughout all eternity. However strongly our sense of justice urges us, as it did all the ages past, to punish wrongdoing, we have learned more and more to realize that the penalty should not be inflicted for the sake of retaliation or revenge, but that it must have the betterment of the individual or the welfare of society in view, and be corrective rather than destructive. Still more must the punitive justice of God have the improvement of man for its purpose, or else it would be cruel and unworthy of God. Yet such would be an endless punishment. It makes God, the Father of mankind, the most cruel tyrant. Endless joy, too, as a reward for the good is unbearable, unless it has an ennobling and salutary effect.

But after all, threats and bribes are at best pedagogic methods for children, not for men. True morality must do away with all selfish motives. The good ought to be done for its own sake, and evil be shunned because it is evil. Says Antigonos of Soko, a Jewish sage of the second pre-Christian century, "Be not as slaves that serve their master with a view to recompense, but be as slaves that serve their master without a view to recompense, and let the fear of God be upon you" (Sayings of the Fathers i, 3). That is to say, serve God from pure motives, in disinterested love of duty. Another teacher in the same treatise (iv, 5) says, "The reward of welldoing is welldoing, and the compensation of evildoing is evildoing." That is, virtue is its own reward, and vice is its own punishment; the one enriches, the other hardens and impoverishes the soul. To both St. Louis and St. Theresa a vision is ascribed, found also in rabbinical writings, of a stately woman striding along the earth with a pitcher of water in one hand and a torch or a bundle of brushwood in the other. "With this one," she said, "I shall quench the fire of hell, and with the other I shall set fire to Paradise," so as to banish self-interest from the hearts of those that do good and avoid evil. Genuine religion fears not hell, but wrongdoing and falsehood, and longs not for heaven, but for goodness and righteousness.

But, then, this is no longer the religion of a single creed or sect, but that of humanity. Such broadness of view could not be expected of Dante, who looked out upon the world with the eyes of a Roman Catholic, and tenaciously clung to the traditions of the Holy Roman Empire. He was broad-minded enough not to share the medieval hatred of the Jew. As he entertained a warm personal friendship for his Jewish contemporary, Immanuel of Rome, the Hebrew poet who became his enthusiastic admirer and skillful imitator in a Hebrew poem on Hell and Paradise, so he obviously had a high regard for the Jewish people. Writing at a time when the great martyr race was made the target of contumely and scorn, the victim of persecution over all the lands, the lofty-minded poet refrained from consigning any of the same to his Inferno, whether among the heretics and schismatics or among the criminals, and he rather spares or pities the Jewish people when referring to the Crucifixion (Inf. xxiii, 126; Par. vi, 45). Nay, he admonishes his Christian fellow citizens not to give cause by brutish behavior to "the mockery of the Jew who dwelleth in their streets" (Par. v, 81). Still he did not learn from his Jewish friend, Immanuel, the traditional rabbinical maxim that "the righteous of all nations have a share in the world to come." The words of the Hebrew poet of "Hell and Paradise" are worth reproducing. Having Daniel—some find here a literal allusion to the name of Dante!—as his guide, he says: "As we were coming through the avenues of Paradise, looking at the group of wise men adorned with beauty, majesty, and dignity in the company of the angels, I asked my guide who they were, and he told me that they were heathen men of wisdom and piety who had rejected the beliefs and ways of their fathers, and risen to the recognition of God as the Fountain of all life and light. And they said, 'By whatever name the Supreme Being may be called by the various nations, we believe in Him who was, is, and shall ever be, who created and rules the world, Himself hidden from sight and beyond all ken, and whose compassionate love encompasses all His creatures, watching them, as the shepherd does his flock, to gather them at the end, and receive them in glory.'"

Neither, apparently, did Dante become acquainted with the parable of the three rings taken from an older Jewish work and based upon an authentic fact, with which a Jewish sage answered the delicate question, put to him by the ruler, as to which of the three religions, the Christian, the Mohammedan, and the Jewish, was the best. It implied the simple truth that the best religion is the one which induces men best to promote the welfare of their fellow-men. In using this parable, borrowed from Boccaccio, Lessing made his Nathan the Wise preach to Sultan Saladdin the grand lesson of religious toleration. Lessing himself, however, was not aware of the fact that, when placed in a similar precarious situation as was his Nathan the Wise, by Don Pedro the Elder of Aragon, at the beginning of the twelfth century—through the question as to which religion was the better one, the Christian or the Jewish—the Jewish sage, Sancho, told him the story of two precious stones given by a father to his two sons, each of whom claimed to possess the more precious one, the jeweler alone being able to decide, and then he closed with the pointed remark that God as the Jeweler must be the final judge.

As a matter of fact, it was in the East where the various religions contested for supremacy, that wise rulers were led to a kind of Deism which advocated toleration, if not equality for each. As early as the ninth or tenth century the Mohammedan rulers at Bagdad held religious disputations of the representatives of the various sects, Christian, Mohammedan, and Jewish as well as Persians, Hindus, and freethinkers, which resulted in the recognition of a common religion of humanity, based on reason and ethics.[1] If not Dante, then at least his authority, Thomas Aquinas, might have caught something of that broader spirit from the Jewish philosophers, such as Ibn Gabirol, whom he knew through a Latin translation. But the Church dogma once for all shut the gate of salvation to those doomed by their "unbelief." Neither Job and Enoch, nor Malachi's verse, "For from the rising of the sun even unto the going down of the same My name is great among the nations" (i, 11), would teach the Churchmen the

---

[1] See Alfred v. Kremer, "Die herrschenden Ideen des Islams," p. 241 ff, and Kohler, "Jewish Theology," p. 430 f.

contrary. Yea, the very words of Jesus (John xiv, 3), "In my father's house there are many mansions," could not plead for a broader conception of religion. It required the enlightenment of a new era to take the bandage from the eyes of the people, to make them see God enthroned in every human heart that strives for righteousness, be it in larger or smaller circles, and to realize that there is no hell but wickedness, and no heaven but goodness and love. As Huxley, the great scientist, despite his agnosticism, well said, "Religion has for all time been best defined by the prophet Micah (vi, 8) in the words, 'It hath been told to thee, O Man, what is good and what the Lord requires of thee but to do justly, to love mercy, and walk humbly with thy God.' "

What especially appeals to us in this and similar utterances of the prophets is the accent laid on social ethics. Religion to these foremost leaders of men is not individualistic in the sense of making the salvation of the soul its sole aim and purpose. Its main object must be the salvation of humanity, the welfare and happiness of the entire social life of men. In the pursuit of social justice and redeeming love we emulate God, the loving Father of men, and by a life of disinterested, self-sacrificing service we approach Him more and more who is the supreme Source and Ideal of love and holiness. This optimistic, prophetic view of life which makes us all coworkers of God is in full consonance with our modern world view, and strongly contrasts with that other-worldliness which found its climax in the medievalism of the "Divine Comedy."

Nevertheless, there is much for us to learn from

Dante's immortal poem. It is the profound and genuine religious spirit which pervades it, the spirit of faith, the yearning for the living God, which made him the prophet of his time. For is not man, as was the Italian bard, again lost in a dark and dense forest, beset with savage beasts of prey, such as are lust and greed, passion and pride, to infest his road of life? Excessive recourse to reason has robbed many of their faith, and daring trust in our mental powers alone has too often cast aside reverence and awe. We are passing amidst severe tests and trials from the former religion of servility and blind authority-worship to one of independent thinking and free manhood, yet while the rod of infernal chastisement and the enticement of paradisiacal bliss have lost their power and influence upon us, the fear of God has likewise been dropped from the heart, and with it also heedfulness to the call of duty. We are in the birth-throes of a new era of humanity, spoken of in the New Testament as well as in the Talmud. The fear of old is gone, and the love of God has not taken its place as yet. Doubt and denial have sapped the very pillars of society and undermined the conscience, the sense of responsibility and dignity which were safeguarded by the old faith. Hence the great crisis we are undergoing in these days. It is our purgatory. We must be reborn to a new faith in God and man. We need a new inspiration, a new interpretation of the ancient truths, a powerful vision which points not to a realm beyond the grave, but beckons us, as did the prophets of yore, forward to a life of duty and service, and makes us all, be it through the Church or the Mosque, the Pagoda or the

Synagogue, partakers of the Kingdom of God, the kingdom of divine justice and love. We must become conscious of our Godlikeness, of the immortality of our spirit which makes us realize that the eternity for which we long in our higher moods is not to begin in another world, but right here and now. Will then our age, strangely divided as it is, between undreamed-of powers of wisdom and humiliating folly, between unheard-of world-embracing philanthropy and fratricidal hatred, see a God-intoxicated seer or singer arise, who will, with Dantelike force and fervor, portray for us the woe and wretchedness of hell in the human breast, to terrify the most abject sinner, and with tears wipe away the stains of guilt from his soul, and also visualize the sublime peace and bliss of heavenly love and righteousness, to fascinate the soul of the most indifferent egoist and fill him with the deepest yearning for God and goodness; one who will say to each and all: Choose between sin and saintliness, between Satan and God? "It is not in the heavens above nor in the far beyond; it is within you, for hand and heart to achieve it!" Somewhere, somehow, his voice will be heard, like Dante's, with its prophetic message of "love, wisdom, and virtue." [2]

[2] Inferno i, 100f (see von Doellinger: "Dante the Prophet" in his Academische Vortraege i, p. 93ff).

B⁻

C

D

Daniel 62

E

Enoch 63 —

Essenes 61

ophecy
Close of 61

R

BL
535
K6

Kohler, Kaufmann, 1843-1926.
    Heaven and hell in comparative religion;
with special reference to Dante's Divine
comedy. New York, Macmillan, 1923.
    xix, 158p. 20cm.

    Includes bibliographical references.

    1. Heaven. 2. Hell--Comparative studies.
3. Dante Alighieri, 1265-1321. Divina commedia.
I. Title.

                                    CCSC/ef